Anna Oppermann

Anna Oppermann
Drawings

Edited by Dan Byers

INVENTORY PRESS

Carpenter Center
for the Visual Arts
Harvard University

This book is published on the occasion of the exhibition *Anna Oppermann: Drawings*, on view at the Carpenter Center for the Visual Arts from June 22 to September 29, 2019.

Editor: Dan Byers
Copy Editor: Eugenia Bell
Audio Transcription: Matteo Cossu
Design: Chad Kloepfer
Publication Coordinator: Carolyn Bailey

Printed and bound in Belgium by die Keure

ISBN: 978-1-941753-32-3
LCCN: 2019948217

Published by
Inventory Press, LLC
2305 Hyperion Ave.
Los Angeles, CA 90027
inventorypress.com

Carpenter Center for the Visual Arts
Harvard University
24 Quincy Street
Cambridge, MA 02138
www.carpenter.center

Distributed by
ARTBOOK | D.A.P.
75 Broad Street, Suite 630
New York, NY 10004
artbook.com

Contents

Introduction

Dan Byers

Anna Oppermann: Drawings brings together a large group of Anna Oppermann's (1940–1993) early drawings and a seminal early installation, an "ensemble" in the artist's words. It is the first solo exhibition of her work in the United States in twenty years. With the exception of a single-work exhibition at P.S.1 Contemporary Art Center, in New York City, in 1999, and the inclusion of her work in the group exhibition *The Everywhere Studio* at the Institute of Contemporary Art, Miami, in 2017, Anna Oppermann's work has been largely invisible in this country. This is the first publication devoted to Oppermann produced in the United States.

Perhaps it is the presence of so much German language in her work that has delayed her reception in the US. With language such an important material and structure to her ensembles and drawings, the inaccessibility to most US audiences must have played a role. (While Oppermann did produce a few works in English, her body of work predates English's dominance of international art discourse.) Yet in this moment of the re-evaluation and recentering of our art histories, it feels as if we might have finally caught up to Oppermann's unique practice. We can see her first-person bodily perspective as it relates to other artists, such as Joan Semmel and Luchida Hurtado, women making work around the same time as Oppermann, whose paintings are receiving a welcome reassessment. And we may see her intimate yet estranging depictions of domestic environments through the lens of younger artists' interest in the body in personal space, from Nicole Eisenman to Jennifer Packer. Further, her proto-internet associative thinking, drawing a vast array of disparate thinkers, images, personal experiences, and discourses into physical proximity through a deeply subjective network of affinity resonates with the hyperlinked associations that structure myriad contemporary "research-based practices."

Beginning in the mid-1960s and through the early '70s, Anna Oppermann created an astonishing series of surreal, almost psychedelic, drawings that uniquely and quietly explode the private space of the home and her experience within it. These early drawings contribute to a feminist reorganizing of spheres traditionally associated with women, casting everyday objects as symbolic, consequential protagonists. Houseplants sprawl to take over and fracture the picture plane, windows and mirrors provide views into other worlds, and tables become small alters or stage sets, displaying drawings that themselves open out into new domestic scenes.

Nearly all of these scenes are presented from the perspective of the artist, clearly indicated by the view of her (or her stand-in's) body as it extends into space, torso and legs foreshortened as she looks down, or knees and feet neatly presented, most often in front of a table. When the body is less emphatically present, it is evoked in abstracted yet corporeal forms or in "ghost images" that frame the views into—and out of—domestic space.

By using her own body as a reference point, Oppermann coaxes the viewer to take on her subjectivity and perspective, emphasizing the gendered realms of the home and the relationships that we form both within and to our private spaces. This first-person perspective inverts the traditional self-portrait, in which the viewer sees the artist's face, presumably either reflected to the artist in a mirror, or rendered from a photograph. In Oppermann's works, mirrors, and actual photographs adhere to the surface of her drawings, populate her drawings as portals or refracting surfaces that reflect the room, rather than the artist. The architecture of the body is woven into the architecture of the room through cross-hatched drawing, swirling forms, and overlapping images. The perspective of this body, synthesized with its surroundings, and the complex array of energy, emotion, and perception that unfolds across each drawing, produces a kind of double empathy, placing the viewer inside artist's body and mind.

I have wanted to organize an exhibition of Oppermann's work for some time. Figuring out the contours and networks around a project often involves talking about it with as many people, in as many contexts, as possible; I was not surprised when I learned that Connie Butler, art historian and Chief Curator of the Hammer Museum at UCLA, was also an Oppermann fan, and had begun research on her work while Chief Curator of Drawings at the Museum of Modern Art in New York. She already had a research file started when I contacted her about contributing to this publication. Here, Bulter contextualizes Oppermann's work within the broader context of international feminist artistic practice in the 1960s and 1970s, a field of research that Butler has generously and rigorously built out through exhibitions and publications over the course of her career.

Art historian, curator, and artist Ute Vorkoeper wrote her dissertation on Anna Oppermann, and worked with the artist toward the end of her life. In addition to other Oppermann projects, Vorkoeper curated the large-scale survey of her work at the Württembergischer Kunstverein Stuttgart in 2007, and (with Herbert Hossman) *Anna Oppermann: Being Different (Why Is She So Different?) 1970–1986* at P.S. 1 Contemporary Art Center in 1999, the artist's only solo exhibition in the US. Vorkoeper's expertise was crucial to this project, working closely with Carpenter Center staff to set up *Being a Housewife*, the early installation which gives an indication of the ways Oppermann's drawings were in dialogue with her early ensembles. Vorkoeper and I recorded the conversation included here, which draws on her direct experience working with Oppermann and our observations and reflections in front of the works themselves, as we installed the exhibition.

Meta Marina Beeck's essay is translated and adapted from her recent text published in the catalogue that accompanied the Kunsthalle Bielefeld's Oppermann exhibition, *Künstler sein* (Being an Artist), on view there in the spring and summer of 2019. Beeck is writing a dissertation on Oppermann's work and used her research into Oppermann's archive to trace a network of influences on the artist's practice—from her biography, popular culture, and her artist peers. The Bielefeld exhibition, organized by Beeck and Kunstalle Bielefeld director Friedrich Meschede, greatly informed my understanding of Oppermann's work and, with its centerpiece ensemble, *Being an Artist*, provides an ideal foil to our centerpiece ensemble, *Being a Housewife*, together invoking the philosophical tension and complex subjectivities expressed in Oppermann's practice.

The ensemble *Being a Housewife* (1968/1973) importantly connects Oppermann's drawing practice to the room-filling, image-based installations for which she would become best known.

Combining large drawings, photographs of drawings, and photo-canvases of displays of drawings and more photographs in space, alongside actual objects, the artist borrowed equally from the display methods of museums, informal memorials, home interiors, and retail to create her ensembles, which were on view in major international exhibitions including the Paris, Venice, and Sydney biennials (1975, 1980, and 1984, respectively) and documenta 6 (1977) and 8 (1987). By focusing on her drawings, the foundational works that would influence the themes and lexicon of the large-scale installations later in her career, *Anna Oppermann: Drawings* lays the groundwork for another institution to take up the task of producing a full retrospective of this remarkable artist.

Castles in the Moon: Anna Oppermann's Aesthetics of Flux

Connie Butler

> This book seems to have a happy beginning. It will have a confusing middle and no discernible end. It just goes on from here to here, dotting the voids. Follow the dots and all you get is lives.[1]
>
> —*Lucy Lippard*

> Castles in the air,
> Just bring worries my love.
> Don't fly, stay down there,
> Your place is on the earth.[2]
>
> —*Frau Luna*

In 1970, the art historian and curator of avant-garde art Lucy Lippard authored a work of fiction. Before becoming known as the author of numerous art historical texts, including the first history of so-called concept art (*Six Years: The Dematerialization of the Object of Art from 1966–1972*), she withdrew from downtown New York's art circles and retreated to Spain, where she spent three months inventing an experimental work of fiction titled *I See/You Mean*. Marshaling her deep knowledge of conceptual art's inquiry into the photographic image, Lippard constructed her novel around the deconstruction of a photograph.

1 Lucy Lippard, *I See/You Mean* (Los Angeles: Chrysalis Books, 1979), p. 3.

2 Oppermann quotes from Paul Lincke's popular opera Frau Luna, in her ensemble *Portrait of Mr. S.* (1969–89). See *Anna Oppermann: Ensembles 1968–1992*, exh. cat., Württembergischer Kunstverein Stuttgart (Ostfildern-Ruit: Hatje Cantz, 2007), p. 200.

I See/You Mean is a close, first-person textual analysis of a group shot of people on the beach. Although it was published in 1979, it was written the same year that Adrian Piper's photographic essay "Groups" appeared in an exhibition curated by Lippard and in a subsequent issue of *Studio International* that she guest-edited. Lippard's *I See/You Mean* anticipated other conceptual works of visual art, such as Allan Sekula's *Meditation on a Triptych* (1973–78), in which the artist narrates three vernacular photographs as if they were seventeenth-century vanitas paintings. The organizing prompt of Lippard's *Groups* exhibition was that each participating artist would photograph a group or groups of people, known to the artist or not, every day for a week. Piper photographed a group of five friends (*Untitled: Groups*, 1969) in her loft over the course of the week and then wrote a description as a response to the exercise. Giving herself a similar set of rules to generate her novel, Lippard deployed a photographic image to catalyze the narrative of the book. The writerly device and conceptual art trope propels the unfolding, fragmentary narrative of anonymous characters A through F. The text is written through a kind of forensic unpacking of the images in the format of a slide show, with each image described in great detail. This kind of operation enacts, of course, the aesthetics of administration that became a hallmark strategy of conceptual art and of Lippard's early (in the history of conceptual art) attempt at applying its methodology and artifice to her creative writing as she had to her curatorial work.

It is also emblematic of a nascent feminist conceptual language. The breaking of form to find the meaning in an image, the interrogation of the ways in which art history traditionally understood representation, was a rupture that has parallels in art practice circa 1970. Like many of her women artist peers, Lippard turned to an alternative form to find a vehicle for a more expressive, more personal voice. In Lippard's case it was academic art writing that she rejected in favor of something potentially more expansive and elastic, a form more accountable to the subjectivities of her own, and eventually, other women's lives. Of course, this is also the story of feminism and the raising of consciousness that was common to the many women artists of Lippard's generation, to whom she finally turned her curatorial attention in 1970. It was also the year she claimed feminist politics and the conflation of these two discoveries—her personal politics and the profound shift in her writerly voice—fortified her strong belief in the impossibility of excising

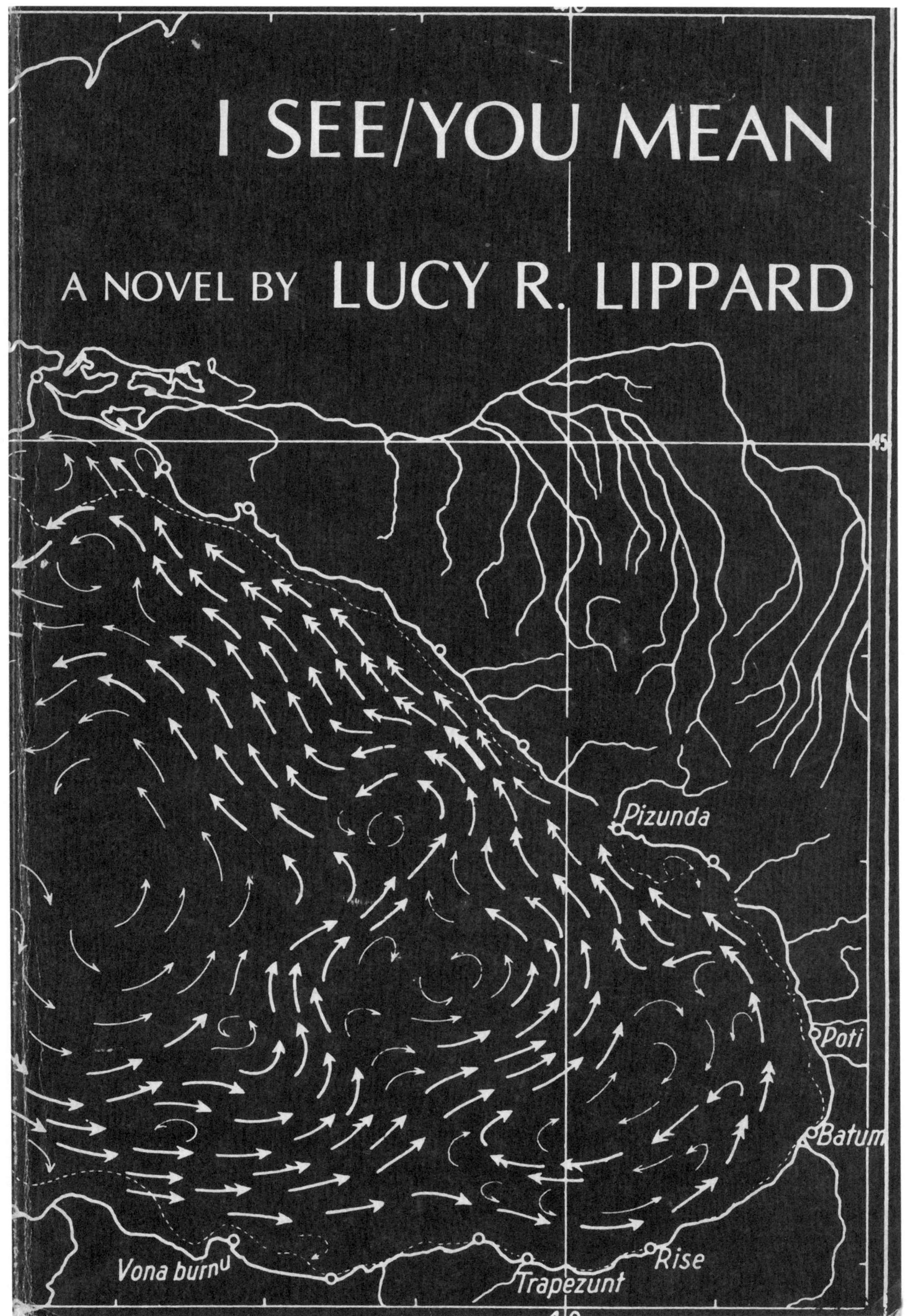

FIG. 1 Lucy R. Lippard, *I See/You Mean*, 1979. Book cover. Los Angeles: Chrysalis Books.

subjectivity.[3] From this moment forward, the personal was political and there was no turning back from life as a subject.

* * *

In 1968 Anna Oppermann, a painter just embarking on her art career in Hamburg, Germany, made a radical break with her pop inspired canvases and moved aggressively off the wall to create an installation she titled *Being a Housewife* (1968–73). An accumulation of drawings, photographs, household plants, and other found, domestic objects, this tableau was oriented on the wall but extended, alter-like onto the gallery floor, adjacent corner, and baseboard, ignoring the conventions of painting but embracing instead some of the more dispersed and discursive impulses of post-minimalist sculpture and performance art. Initiating her field of activity for collecting and constructing *Being a Housewife*, with a poetic set of themes and key words, "being a housewife, being normal, my perfect dream house, naive woman, smart woman deprivation, letters, repression, bunny on eggs," as well as references to the plants, "cactus, grass lily, calla, hazelnut."[4] The lists like this one that Oppermann used to generate some of her works lay bare the contradictions of a woman's life and artistic practice, and the double consciousness of W. B. Dubois that was taken up not only by black intellectuals and artists during the civil rights era to describe their experience of racism, but also by women artists to describe the oppressive condition of working both under and outside of the male gaze. Over and over again in the history of feminist art there are stories of women finding voice outside of the restrictive conventions of marriage and home, and constructing new identities as practicing artists. Self-construction, through the practice of art, both as a subject and operating methodology, is fundamental to defining a feminist conceptual idiom.

Being a Housewife is a fragile accumulation. That is, it lacks the formal confidence which accrued to Oppermann's installations over time as she figured out how to create an architecture for her networked imagery and collections of material. Though emerging out of a traditional painting training, she was part of the resurgence

3 See my *From Conceptualism to Feminism: Lucy Lippard's Numbers Shows 1969–1974* (London: Afterall Books, 2012), pp. 50–51.

4 Herbert Hossmann, "Anna Oppermann's Ensembles: An Annotated Index," in *Ensembles*, p. 241.

of surrealism in pop inspired imagery that happened internationally in the 1960s, and found her methodology as an artist through a desire to manifest her life by making visible a set of emotions and relationships. This is the erotics of her art. In early works such as *Being a Housewife*, her impetus appears to explode the confines of painting by drawing, redrawing, and photographing to create what looks like an elaborate storyboard, a diaristic array of notes and images from her life and her art. Casual photographs of all kinds are informally taped to the wall, spread on a makeshift table, and leaned against the floorboards and reveal of the gallery, ignoring the dictates of gallery convention. There is an almost childlike demand for the viewer's attention, to synthesize the information so forensically presented. This layering of material and reference to create a visual narrative is highly personal, but also highly contingent on correlative moments in the real world of news, politics, and daily life—those moments that mark an image with specificity and meaning that Roland Barthes called the punctum of the photographic image.

Snapshots are littered throughout Oppermann's works, literally creating a kind of black-and-white (and sometimes, rarely, color) field of flickering and leaking information that at once invites a conversation and resolutely obfuscates or frustrates a coherent one from occurring. There are fragments of text, glimpses of advertising, and images of things we are looking at: notes, drawings, and objects, even as we look at them. The cover of Oppermann's exhibition catalogue, *Ensembles 1968–1992*, shows the artist kneeling among her own snapshots and drawings, a Leica camera focused downward at the array, presumably photographing and rephotographing her own images. This simultaneity of vision is one of the most disorienting aspects of the artist's work. The dysphoria located in a network of images that refuses to cohere is an effect that the artist built in to the methodology of her work. In copious journals, artist and psychoanalyst Bracha Ettinger has written about the "state of multiplicity as a starting point" for the making of art.[5] Theoretically Oppermann anticipates Ettinger's matrixial web which she describes, "… an unconscious space of simultaneous emergence and fading of the I and the unknown non-I; it is a shared borderspace in which differentiation-in-co-emergence and distance-in-proximity are continuously

[5] Bracha Ettinger, quoted in Catherine deZegher, "Drawing Out Voice and Webwork," in *Art as Compassion: Bracha L. Ettinger* (Brussels: ASA Publishers, 2011), p. 136.

rehoned and reorganized by metamorphosis."[6] A child of Holocaust survivors, Ettinger's own visual art combines a kind of abstraction extracted from the blending of the autobiographical and the space and imagery of historical memory. Like Oppermann, her conflation of these two image sources intentionally blurs the space of autobiography.

In Oppermann's *Being a Housewife*, a kind of matrixial thinking is evident even as the artist is working out her form. Images are born from one another, decentering and disallowing any one focal point or point of origin, to develop. In the middle of this work, for example, is a free-standing projection screen, the kind that might be found in classroom. Onto this backdrop is drawn an image of a dollhouse table and chairs, the domestic realm of the housewife in question. The arrangement appears as a drawing, as a photograph, and then in several photographs in which some action has occurred: a little chair is upset, the table appears covered and not, and then animated by little drawings of drawings. The actual dollhouse table and chairs are visible as well amid the accumulation. The kitchen table as a central trope in early feminist imagery is undeniable. For Oppermann it seems to be the site of both the constriction and the undoing of an identity. As it was for many women artists, the kitchen or family dining table itself was often reinvented as a work surface, as the only place in the home, along with the bathroom, where work (and sometimes the privacy necessary to do that work) could be achieved. The relentlessness that accompanied caretaking and domestic labor was frequently mirrored by the restless and furtive productivity of women who found art and began working furiously. While any single focus or attention might have been negated because of the necessities of familial or maternal life, a dispersed or networked kind of attention is reflected in the visual form of the ensemble.

Oppermann's accumulations of material taken from her life and re-sorted into an expanded form of drawing constitute the creation of a studio environment writ large and made public, turned inside out for the viewer to read and decode. Already evident in her large and very colorful, mixed-media drawings of the mid- and late 1960s, which became the formal core of her early installations, is the subject of a multiple gaze. In 1978 the artist described her form and process, claiming the term "ensemble" to describe them: "Ensemble is

6 Ibid., quoted from an undated notebook, p. 117.

the name I give to the documentation of a particular method during perception and/or awareness exercises … The documentation is a visualization, a consciousness, different systems of reference ….”[7] In a text first published in 1979 titled “What is an Ensemble?,” Oppermann describes her process as almost scientific and the ambition for her work as a social and time-based engagement with the viewer.[8] Using language that was ahead of its time in its understanding of the temporal as an active element of her practice, she describes the method of her work and its relationship with the viewer as an event encounter. Her writings reveal a preoccupation with *Alice in Wonderland* and the seduction of the mirror as both a reflection and a window, a way in and an escape from reality and the dimension of the present. The relationship between appearance and reality is the subject of Oppermann's early *Mirror Ensemble* (1968–89), which features several drawn and photographed images of mirrors that together provide a visual architecture for this installation. The coincidence of different systems of reference, of simultaneous views reflecting often contradictory and multiple points of view is visible in the presence of mirrors and windows which populate almost all of the early drawings from 1968. In one group of drawings made from the vantage point of looking down her own body toward her thighs and knees, Oppermann places a small reflective tondo—an image of a mirror or aperture—which appears to open onto another world. In the most ambitious of these very colorful drawings, the scale is large and the artist centralizes the imagery around and emanating from the body. Often the body that is visible is also an extension of some domestic object, anthropomorphizing, for example, an ashtray or can of sardines, making these banal containers protagonists in the drawings, frequently appears. It is as if the artist begins each work from the same place, seated at a dining table that becomes a work surface. In these drawings the space of the table and the space of the body seem to merge, upended to face the viewer, and simultaneously to open up as if an aperture had appeared and opened onto another, private fantasy world.

Like many women artists who felt trapped in the domestic realm and confined by the strictures of motherhood and traditional, heteronormative marriage, and the lack of a non-domestic space to work, Oppermann's is a claustrophobic image world that emanates from

7 *Ensembles*, p. 50.

8 Ibid., p. 112–13.

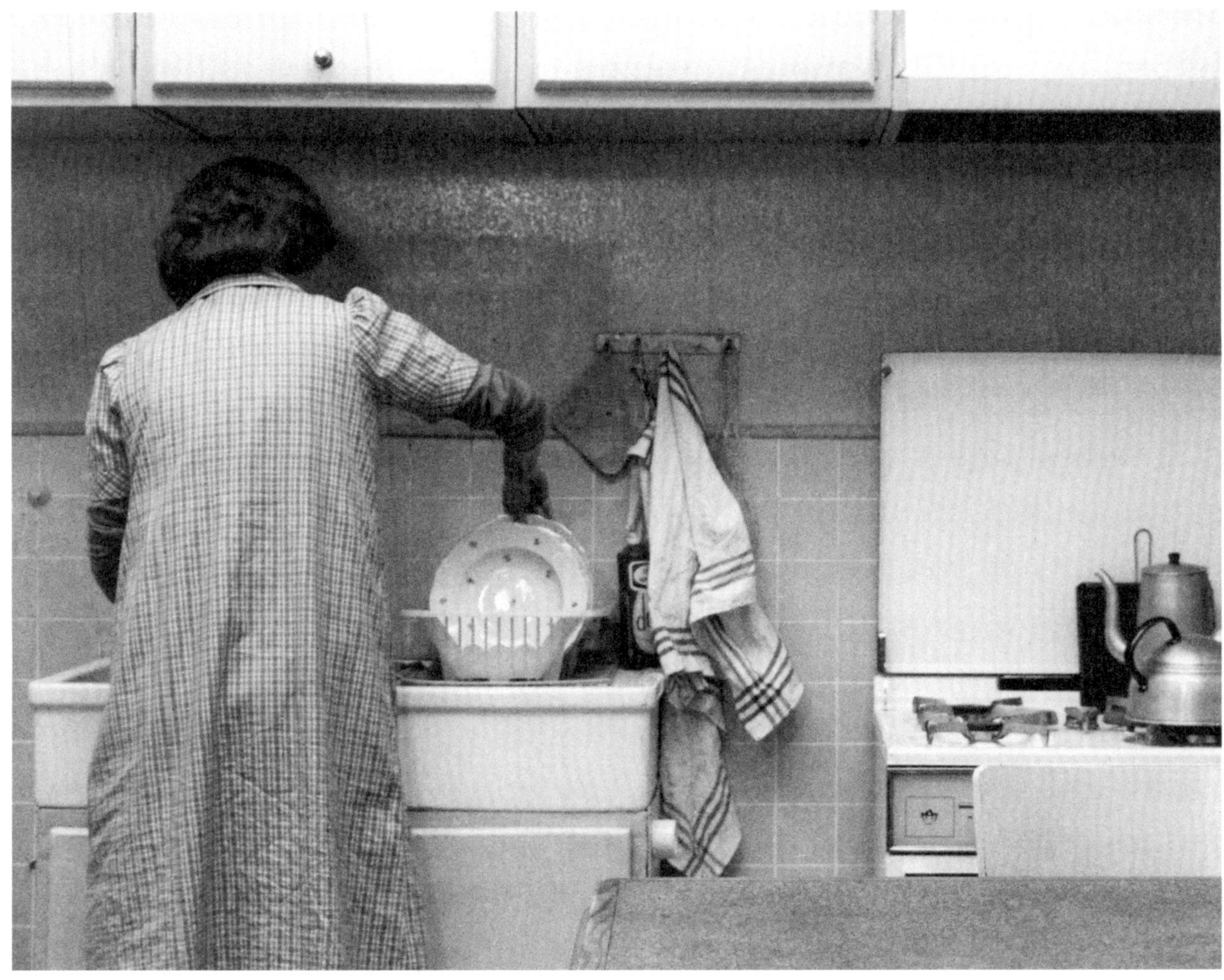

FIG. 2 Chantal Ackerman, still from *Jeanne Dielman 23 Commerce Quay, 1080 Bruxelles*, 1983. 35mm film.

her own body. I am thinking here of early self-images by Joan Snyder of her thighs and torso while seated on the toilet in *Flesh Flocked Painting with Strokes and Stripes* (1970) or Joan Semmel's early erotic images of her own body based on photographs and the gaze of the camera lens. In the European context, artists such as the Belgian Lili Dujourie made intimate videos of her own body reflected in the mirror as she performed the languid poses of a classical female nude. In 1972, her series of five silent video works titled *Hommage a ...*, she poses as a classical female nude, reflecting on the discourses of art history in relationship to voyeurism and the male gaze. In 1975, the Belgian filmmaker Chantal Ackerman made her iconic feminist film *Jeanne Dielmann, 23 Quai du Commerce, 1080 Bruxelles*, which tracks the a day in the life of a woman, a mother, who painfully and slowly cares for her grown son even as she works as a prostitute during the day when her son is away. Shot in real time, in color, the film forensically catalogs her domestic chores and her sex work, and focuses in a non-hierarchical way on the details and brutality of daily existence. Oppermann, too, draws and imagines based on what she encounters in her immediate foreground, albeit run through a near psychedelic and saturated range of colors. In one drawing a pelvis becomes an ashtray. In another the space between the thighs opens onto a telescopic rabbit hole through which small creatures and images appear. These large drawings are almost all symmetrical as if a Rorschach-like depiction of the center of the body conceals and reveals a rich fantasy world within. Oppermann pictures an interior life that is both suffocating and psychedelic and it is these intimate yet hallucinatory and surrealistic drawings which become the foundation for her first ensembles and the *mise en abyme* that she created within each one.

* * *

Beginning a discussion of Oppermann with Lucy Lippard is an intentional invocation of the uneasy relationship between early feminist practice and high conceptual art as it was canonized and circulated between the US and Europe in the first half of the 1970s. While histories of conceptual art also embrace Latin America and Asia, as well as other Anglophone countries, including Canada, the UK, and Australia, the exhibition histories of artists such as Oppermann tend to draw a narrower, Euro-American geography marked by the major cities in Germany, a stint in Paris, and a periodic engagement with the US (usually New York). In many ways the trajectory of Oppermann's remarkable work unfolds as a history not unlike other women artists of her generation who thematized their own lives and identities as artistic strategy. Born in 1940 and living her early years during the most intense bombing and destruction of Hamburg during World War II, she finished art school in 1968, having studied graphic arts and painting at the Hochschule für bildende Künste Hamburg (University of Fine Arts Hamburg). Oppermann then embarked on a radical project of installation and drawing that has defied categorization. Tracing the many ways in which her work is also deeply engaged with questions of the photograph renders it both more contemporary, aligning her vision with artists such as Sarah Sze and Moira Davey, whose work expands the use of the deconstructed photograph as a metaphor, but also has fascinating parallels to the uses of photography during the war. How might we account for a history of photography that encompasses both the aerial photographs used by bomber pilots to identify their targets during World War II and the photographic portrait used to forensically label and codify the identities of thousands of Jews whose lives and tragic deaths indelibly mark the historical memory of Oppermann's generation?

In many ways this fascinating artist has only now found her audience, in part because our own world has become so visually saturated. Oppermann's attempt to represent and inhabit a complex and networked consciousness is perfectly analogous to the multiple attentions, what she called the "polyphonic expansion" of our contemporary moment.[9] The current reception of her work has included young feminist artists and curators, lovers of drawing in the expanded field, and those of us interested in amplifying the under-recognized field of feminist conceptual art. Her work has been written about most convincingly as conceptual art that somehow falls between the theoretical cracks because of the strange and unsettling ways it functions both materially and in the mind of the engaged viewer. More than a few writers have attempted to describe the disorienting experience of viewing Oppermann's installations as impenetrable, simultaneously requiring close viewing and yet resisting a slow read. While the very limited critical literature around

9 Ibid., p. 113.

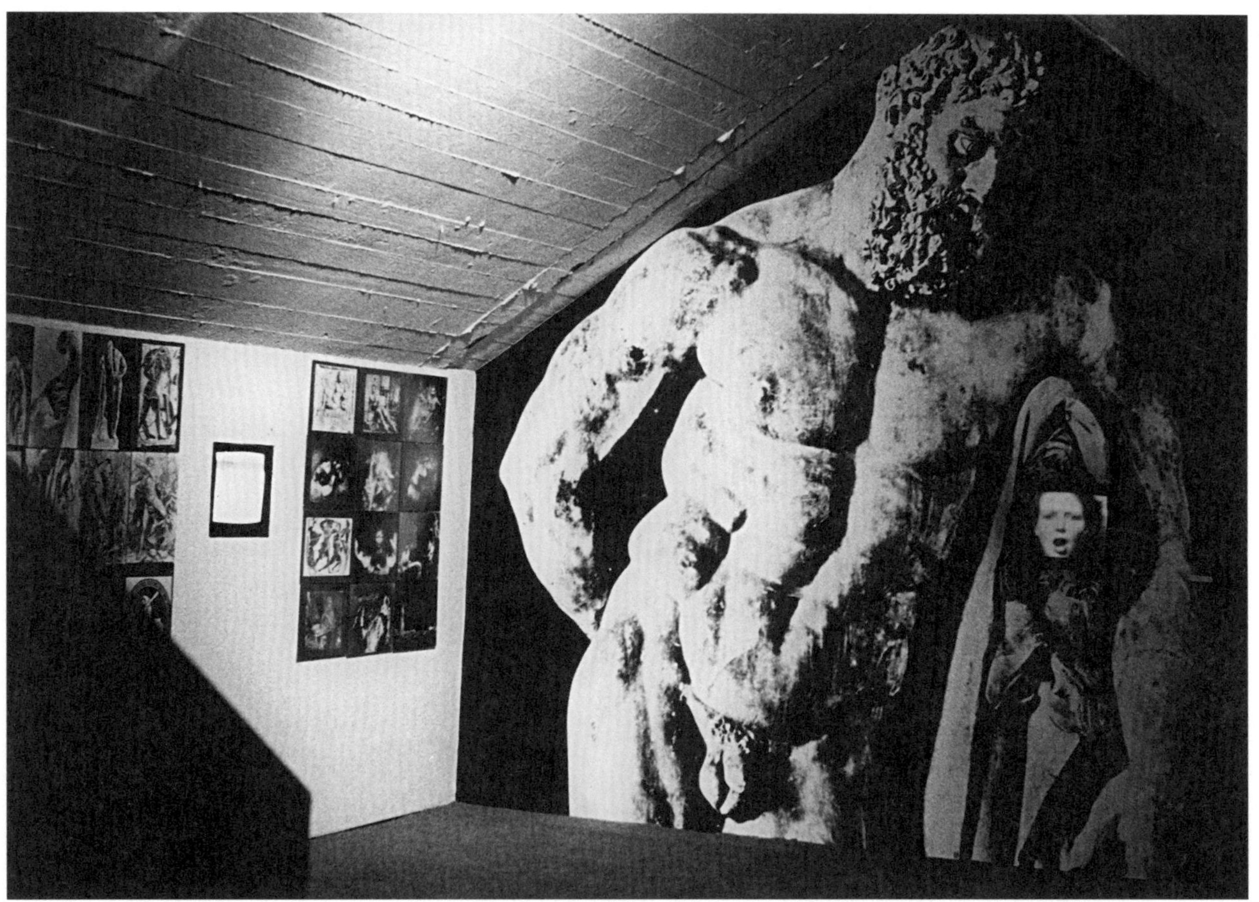

FIG. 3 Ulrike Rosenbach, *Herakles-Hercules-King Kong*, 1977, installation view at *documenta 6*, Kassel, 1977. Mixed media.

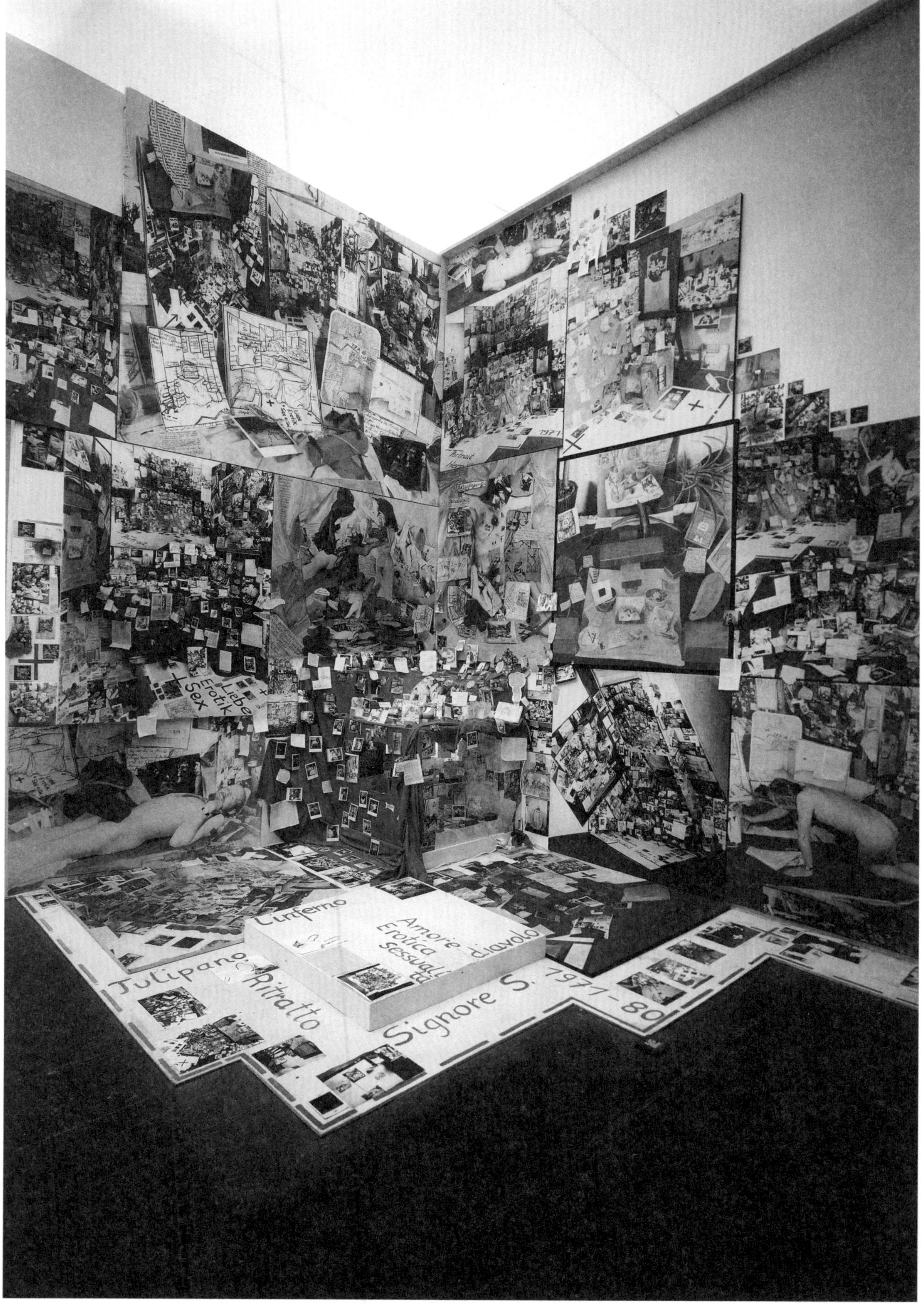

FIG. 4 Anna Oppermann, *Portrait of Mr. S.*, 1969–89, installation view at Hamburger Kunstverein, 1984. Mixed Media.

her work describes it as idiosyncratic and uniquely personal for its time, this language seems to require a critical history that has yet to be written, connecting a handful of German and other European women to their feminist counterparts working internationally. Artists such as Katharina Sieverding, Ulrike Ottinger, and Ulrike Rosenbach, with whom Oppermann participated in documenta 6 in 1977, each moved beyond their foundational mediums of painting or printmaking to invent new languages of installation-based art that could accommodate their desire for a more personal and autobiographical subject. While her colleagues accomplished this through film and video, Oppermann invented a kind of spatial ensemble based in drawing, while incorporating elements of collage, montage, and three-dimensional thinking in the form of maquettes and models. All of these artists were educated and worked, as women, among male peers in an art world that did not and could not accommodate their inventive and ambitious visions. Oppermann's art, and her evolution from surrealism-inspired erotic pop to the production of dispersed installations that function discursively in the space of drawing and even performance, can be understood in a rich, yet loose history of feminist conceptual art that is ripe for mining and as yet unwritten.

* * *

Love, sex, eroticism, devil, hell, heaven, sin, penance, confession, witches, chaos, crucifix, crucifixion, cross, erection, phallus, horse, bedding down, double standards, gap-toothed, San Gimignano, castles in the moon.[10] These are the thematic key-words used by Oppermann to inspire and construct an installation called *Portrait of Mr. S.* (1969–89). The installation existed for three years at Der Teufelhof hotel, in Basel. The artist incorporated the ceiling and walls of a guest room and could be viewed from the bed in the middle of the room. It was installed in a 2019 exhibition titled *Straying from the Line* at the Schinkel Pavillion, in Berlin. Organized by Jenny Nachtigall this exhibition mapped an expanded and heterogenous narrative of feminist encounters and marked the fiftieth anniversary of Lee Lozano's 1969 proclamation that there "can be no art revolution that is separate from a science revolution, a political revolution,

10 Ibid., p. 245.

an education revolution, a drug revolution, a sex revolution or a personal revolution."[11] The show brought together a synthetic and multi-generational group of artists representing a "multiplicity of feminist tendencies."[12] Invoking Lozano's insistence on the disruption of boundaries between art and social life, the 1960s art into life call to arms and the #MeToo movement in its press release, the curator of this exhibition, Nina Pohl, mapped a feminist present for a younger generation. By straying from—indeed resisting, in all kinds of ways—notions of the binary, this curatorial sweep invokes Julia Kristeva's still radical theory of Women's Time. "As for time," she wrote, "female subjectivity would seem to provide a specific measure that essentially retains *repetition* and *eternity* from among the multiple modalities of time known through the history of civilization … this feminism situates itself outside the linear time of identities which communicate through projection and revindication. Such a feminism rejoins, on the one hand, the archaic (mythical) memory and, on the other, the cyclical or monumental temporality of marginal movements."[13]

Oppermann's relationship to the domestic sphere and its exigencies is on bold display in her diffuse installations, which propose the everyday as open conversation. The precarity of the networked, dispersed materiality of her materials contains a proposal about the personal as available and the quotidien as meaningful.

11 From the press release for *Straying from the Line*, Schinkel Pavillon, Berlin, April 13–July 28, 2019, https://www.schinkelpavillon.de/exhibition/straying-from-the-line/.

12 Ibid.

13 Toril Moi, ed., *The Kristeva Reader* (New York: Columbia University Press, 1986), pp. 194–95.

Works

Beans, 1968
Mixed media on Masonite
43 ¼ × 43 ¼ inches (110 × 110 cm)

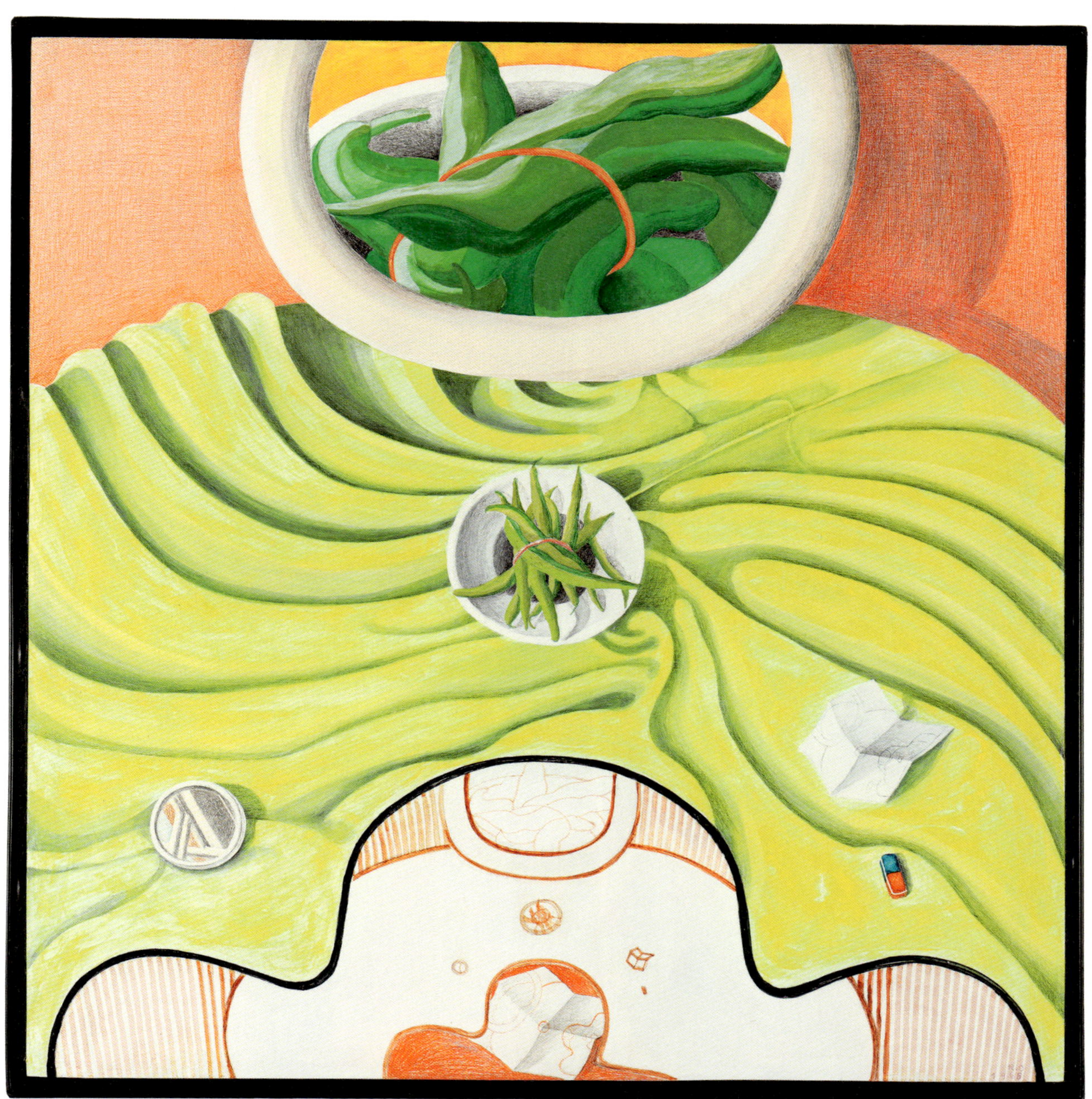

Chives, 1968
Mixed media on Masonite
43 ¾ × 44 inches (111 × 112 cm)

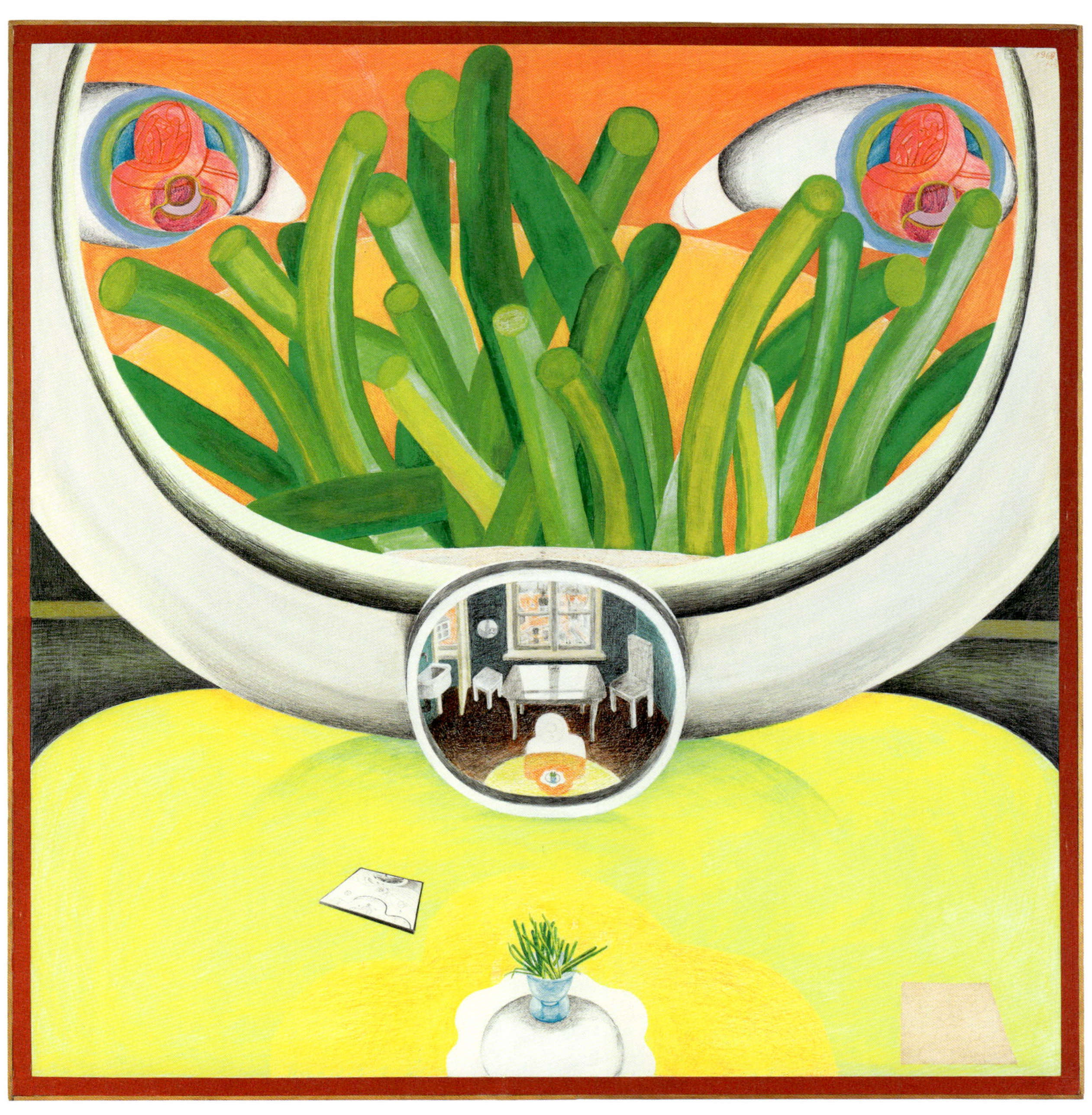

Untitled, 1969
Mixed media on Masonite
51 ⅛ × 47 ¼ inches (130 × 120 cm)

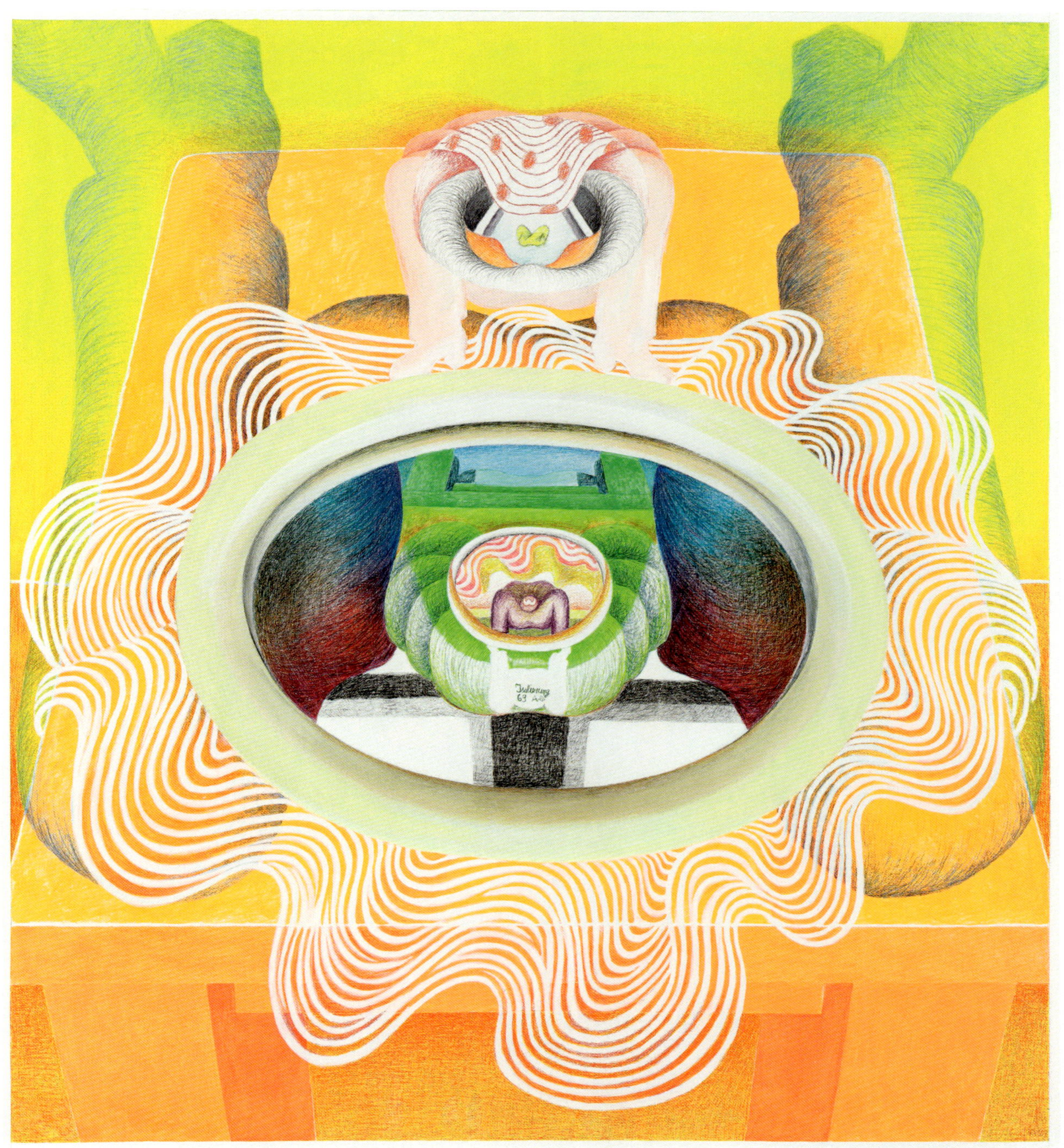

Red figure with curtain, 1968
Mixed media on Masonite
59 × 48 inches (150 × 122 cm)

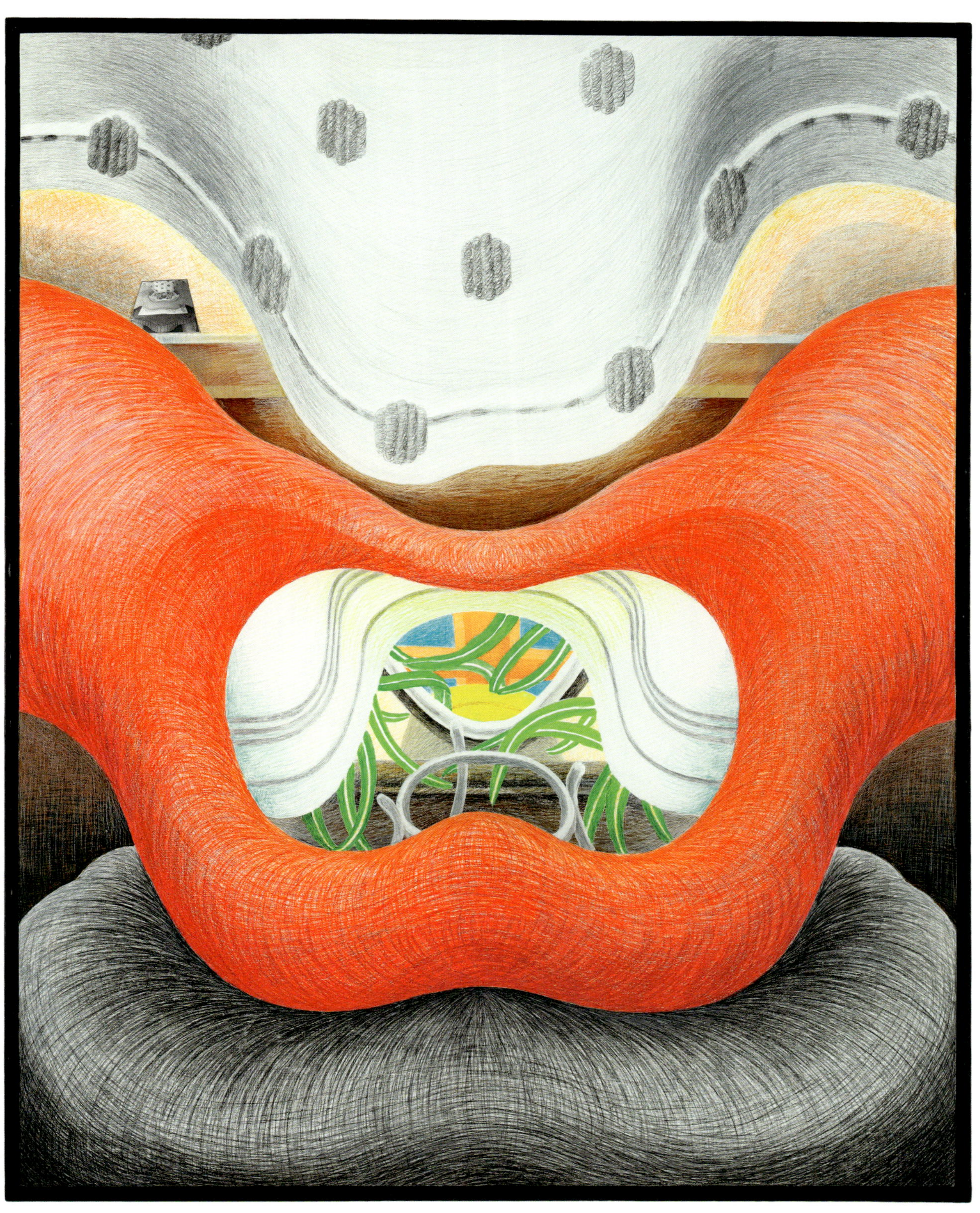

Mirror corner, 1968/1970
Mixed media on Masonite
51 ⅛ × 54 ¼ inches (130 × 138 cm)

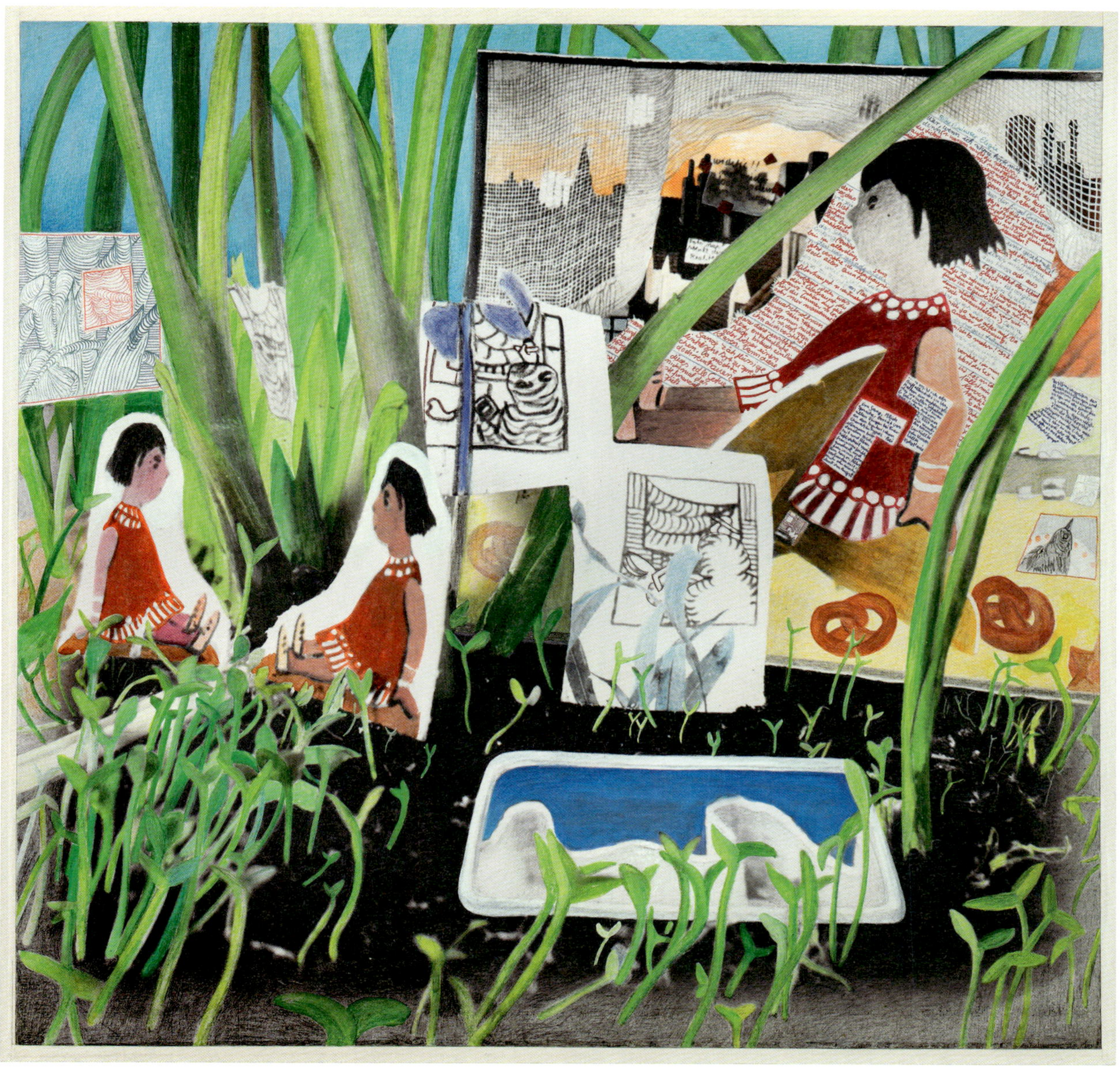

With ashtray, 1968/1970
Part of the ensemble "Antidesign"
Mixed media on Masonite
59 × 48 inches (150 × 122 cm)

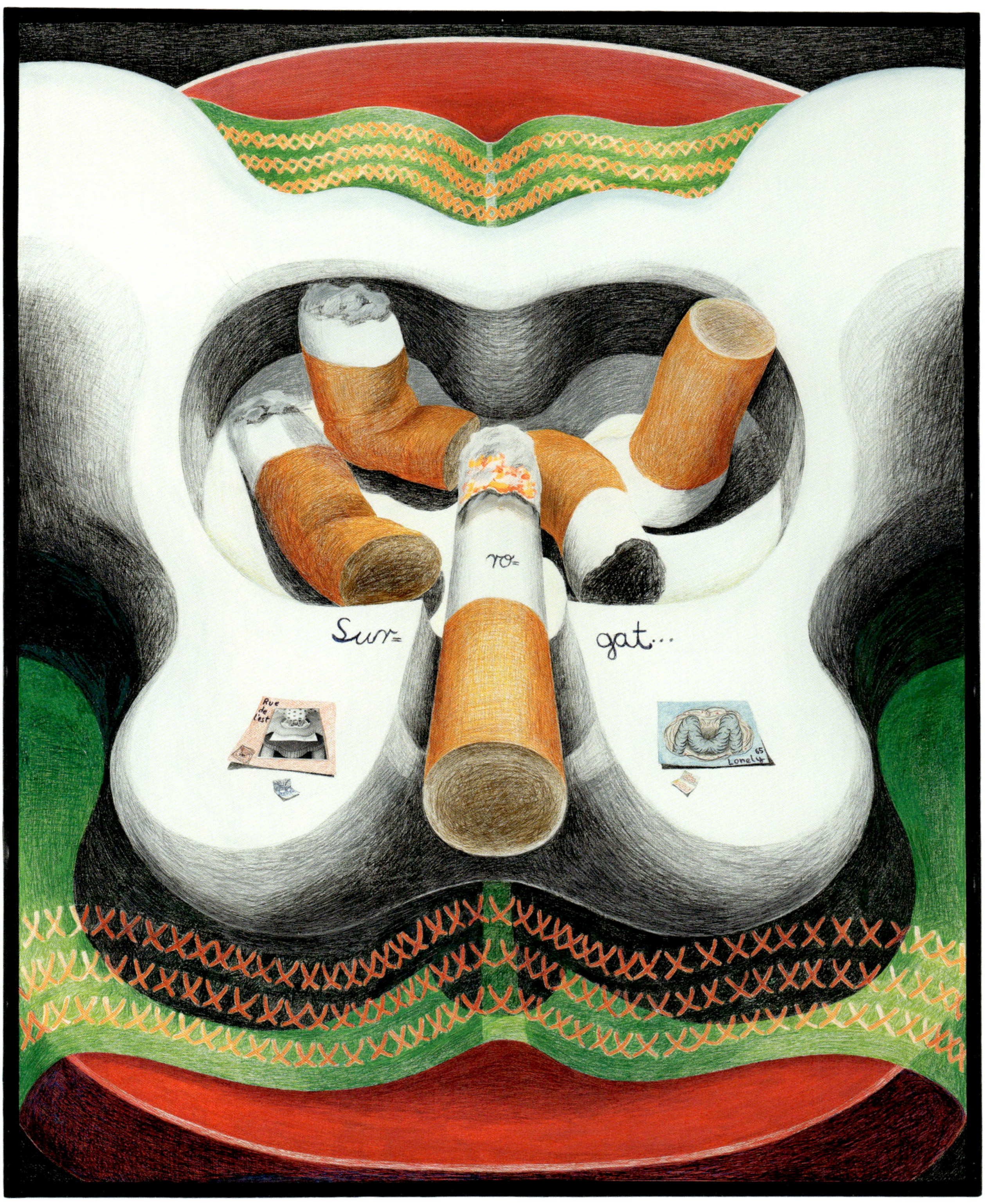
Sur=
ro=
gat...
Rue de l'est
65
Lonely

Untitled, 1970
Mixed media on cardboard
32 ½ × 23 ¼ inches (83 × 59 cm)

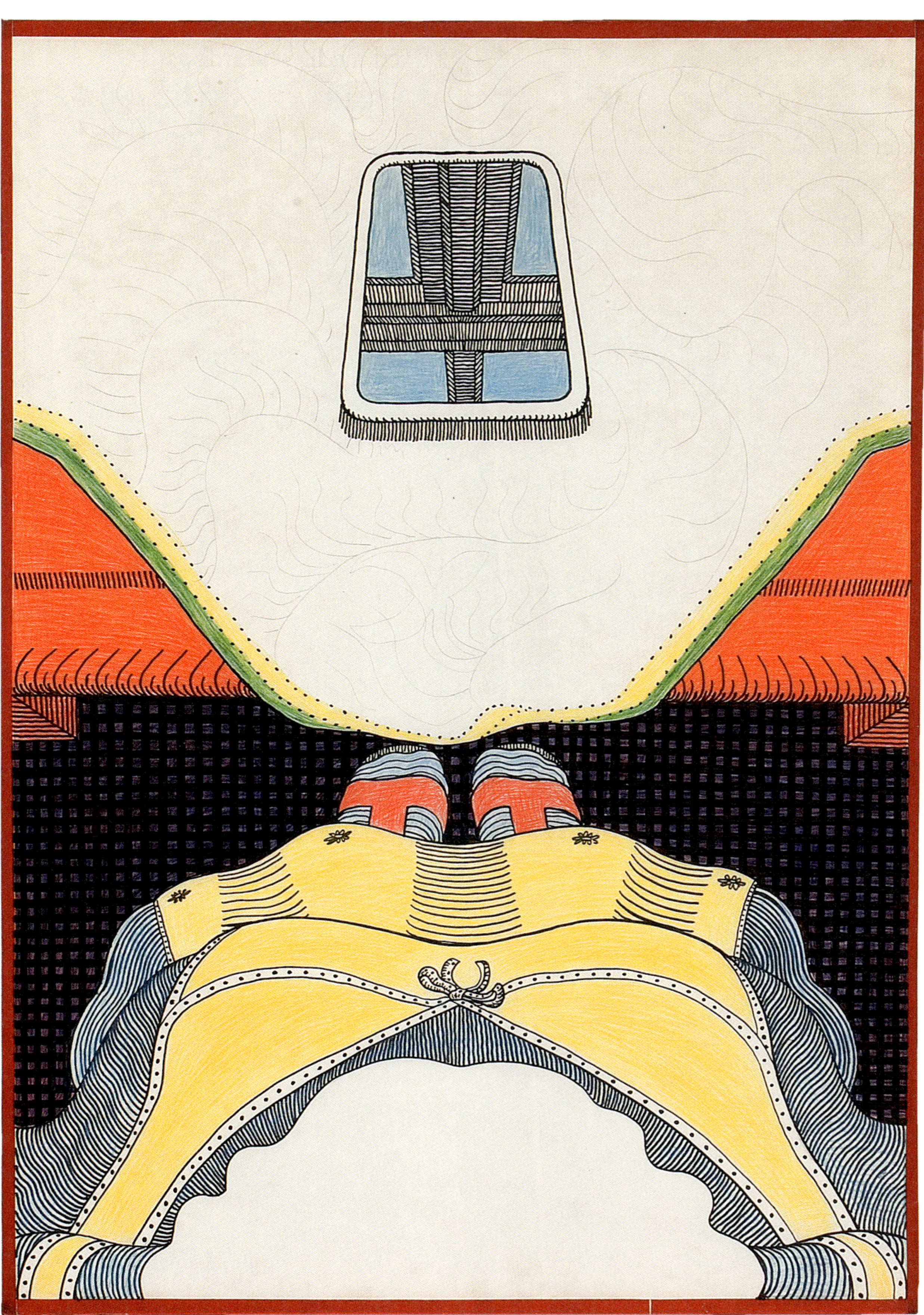

Untitled, 1970
Mixed media on cardboard
33 × 23 ¼ inches (84 × 59 cm)

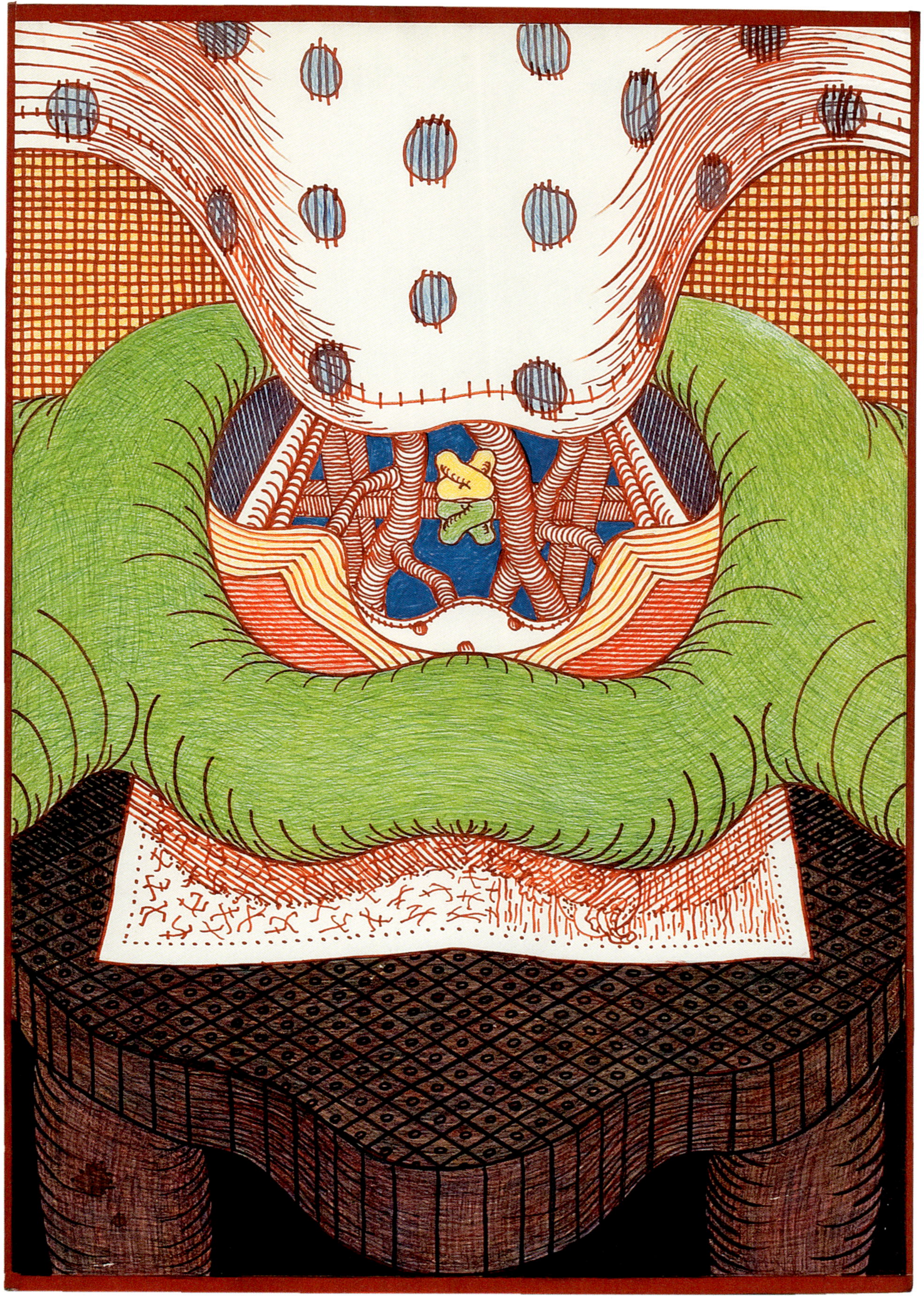

Untitled, 1970
Mixed media on cardboard
33 × 23 ¼ inches (84 × 59 cm)

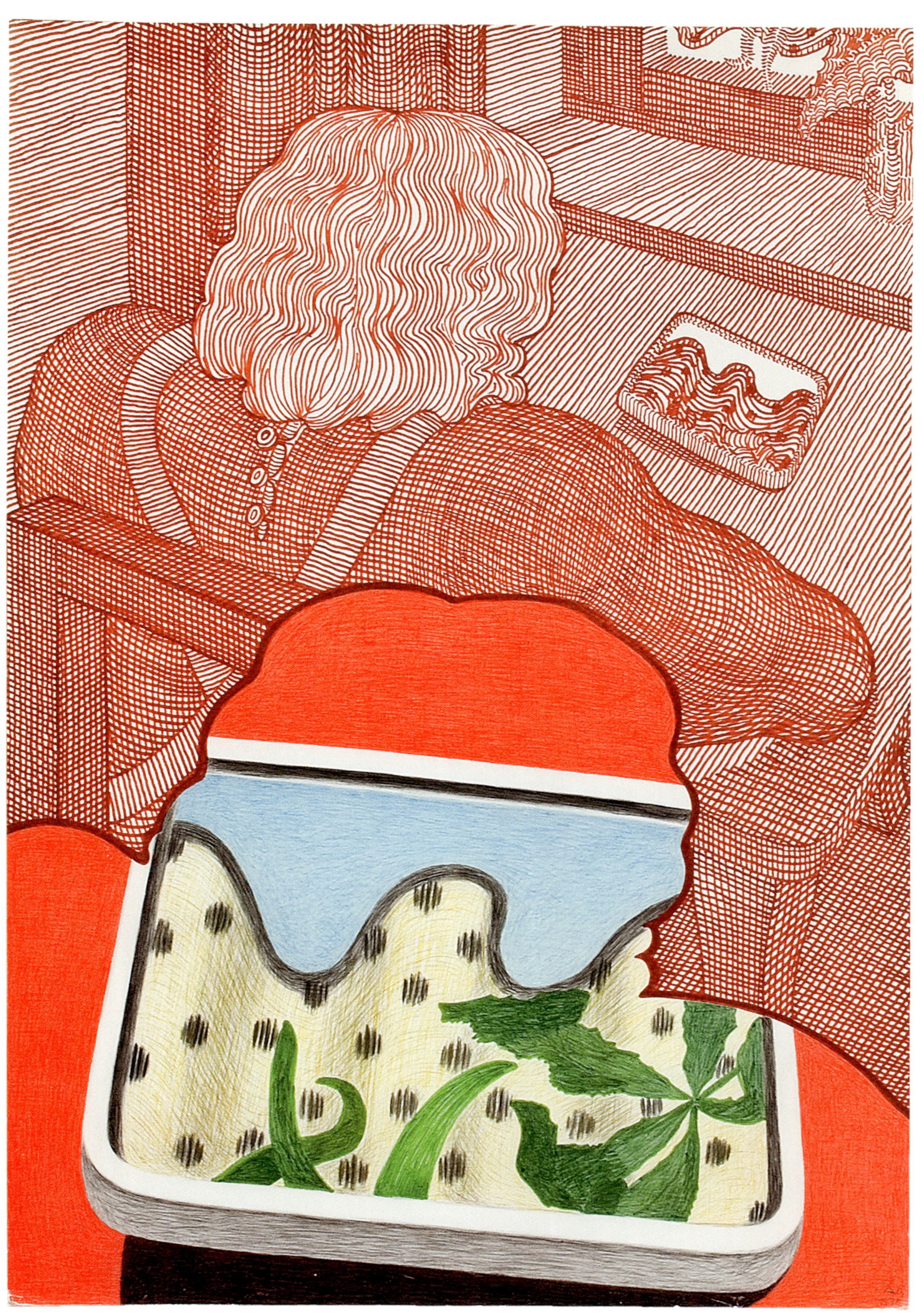

Untitled, ca. 1968
Mixed media on cardboard
19 ¾ × 33 inches (50 × 84 cm)

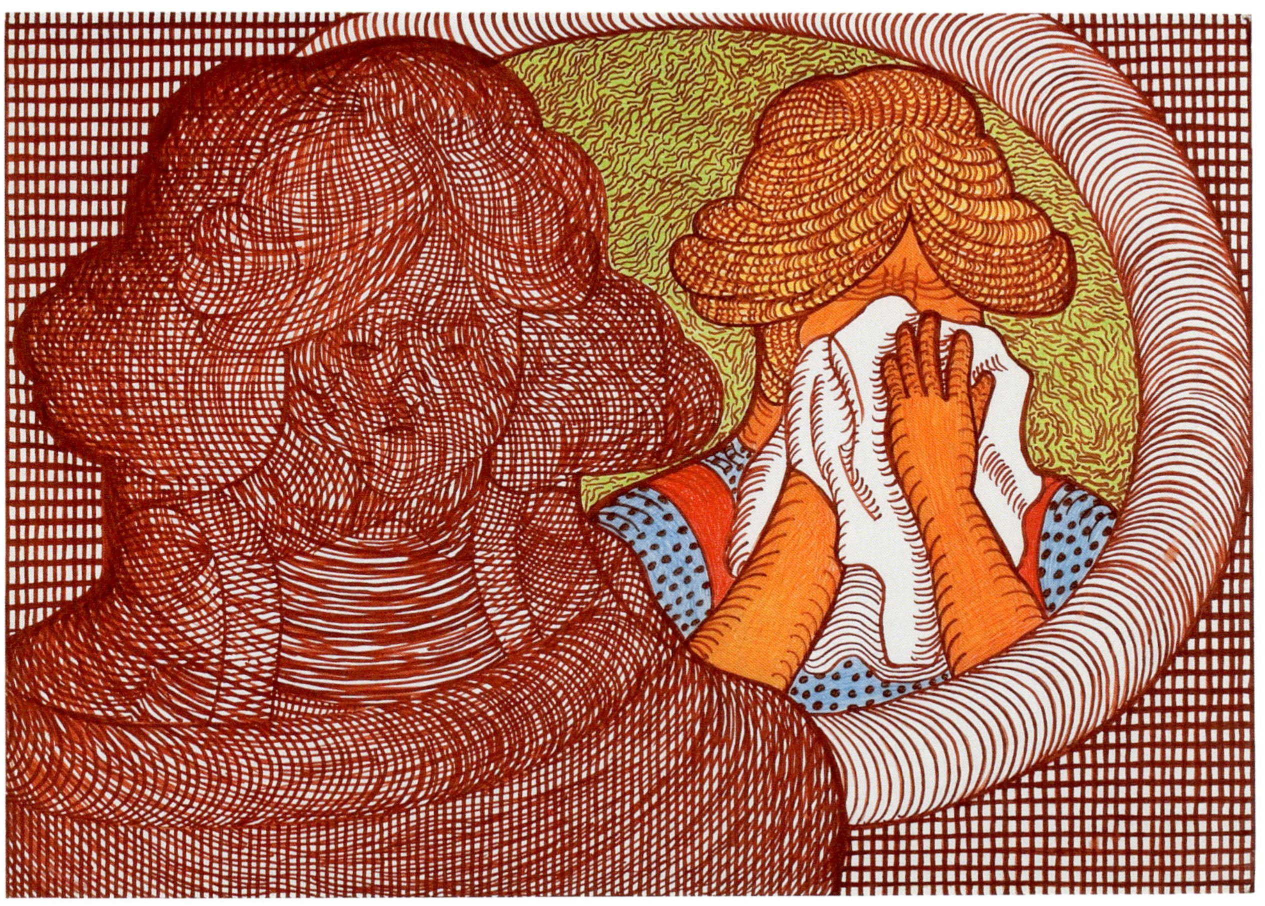

Untitled, ca. 1968/1970
Mixed media on cardboard
33 × 23 ¼ inches (84 × 59 cm)

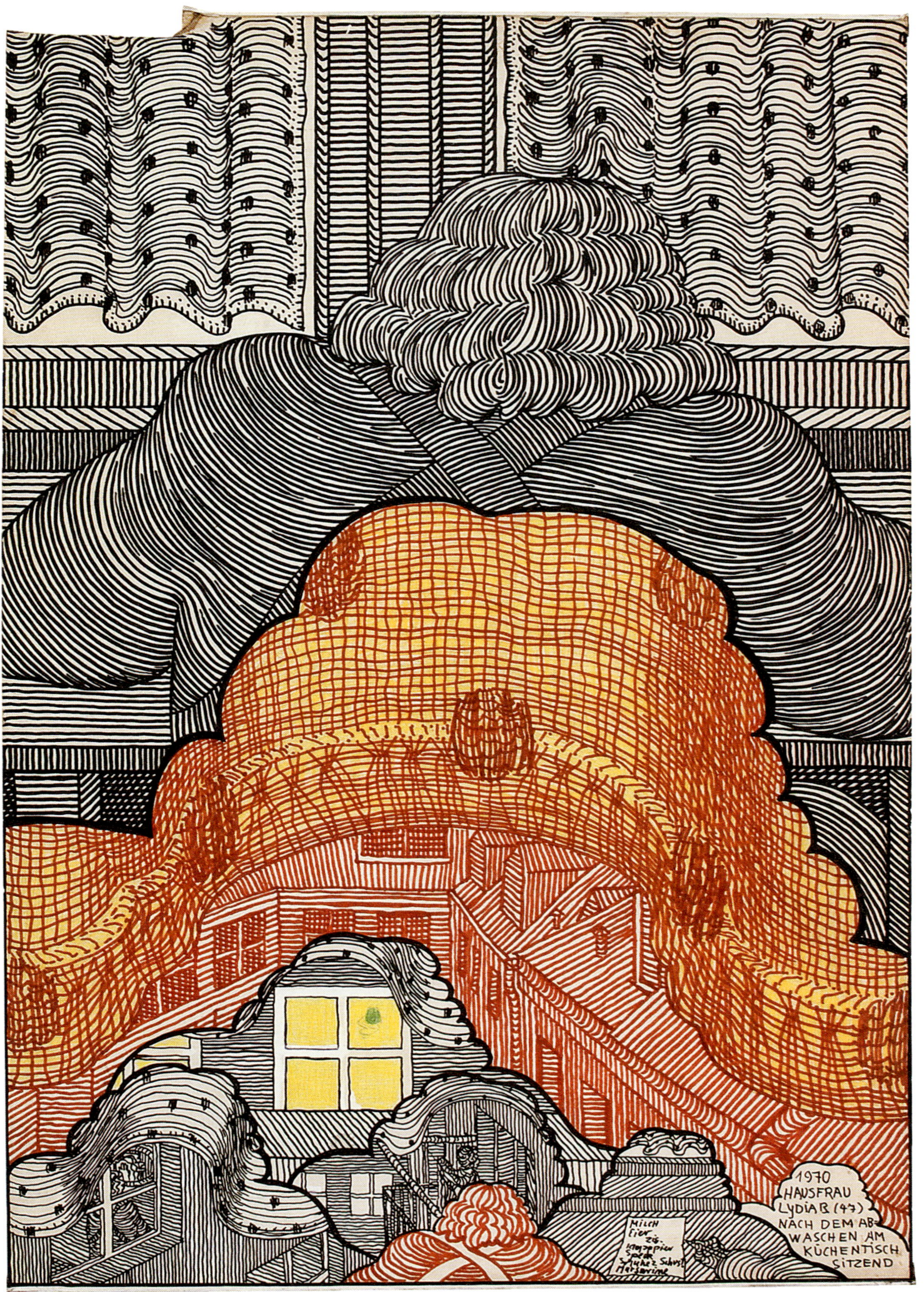
1970 HAUSFRAU LYDIA B (47) NACH DEM ABWASCHEN AM KÜCHENTISCH SITZEND
MILCH
EIER

Untitled, 1970
Mixed media on cardboard
33 × 23 ½ inches (84 × 60 cm)

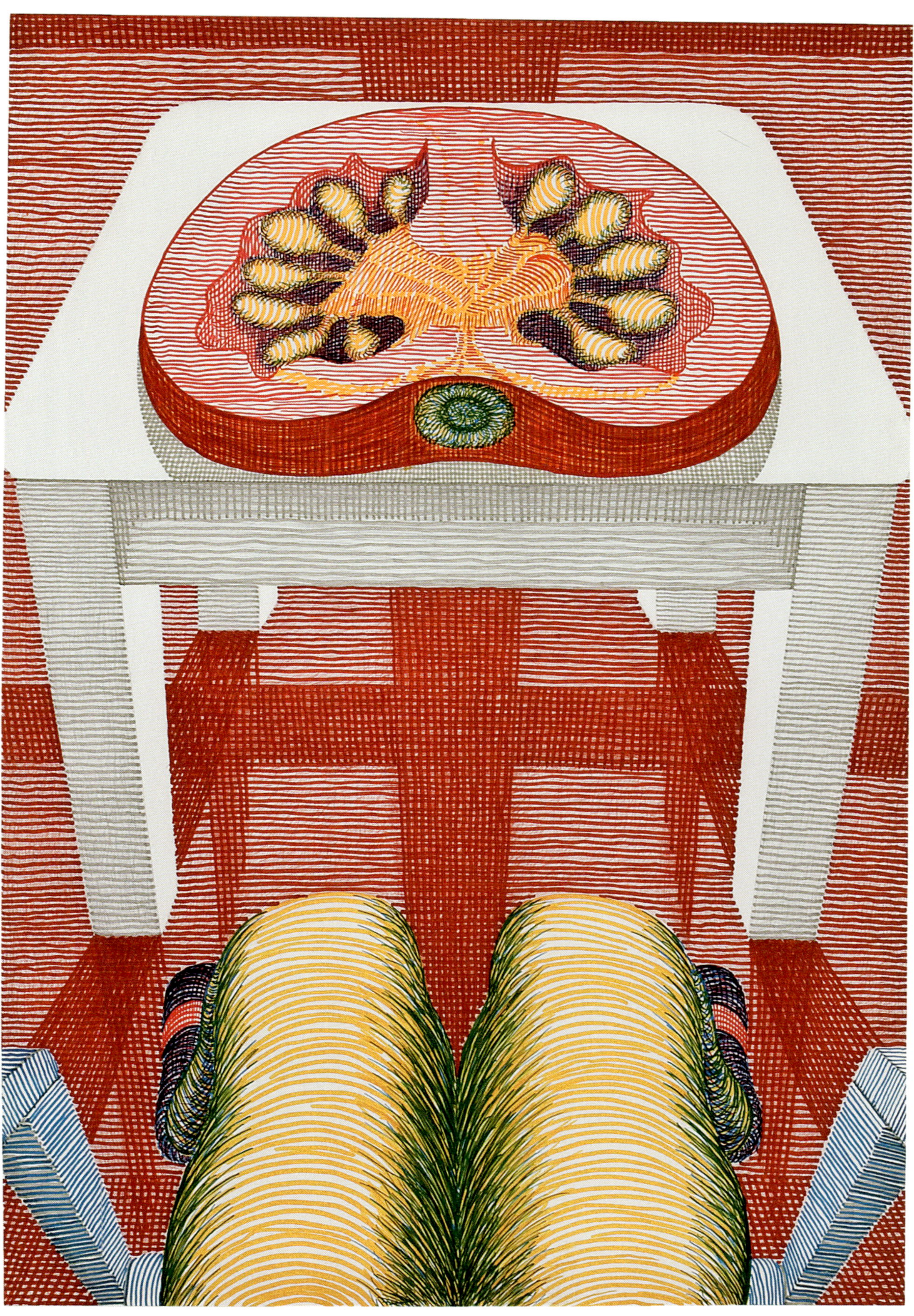

Untitled, ca. 1968
Mixed media on cardboard
32 ¾ × 23 ¼ inches (83.5 × 59 cm)

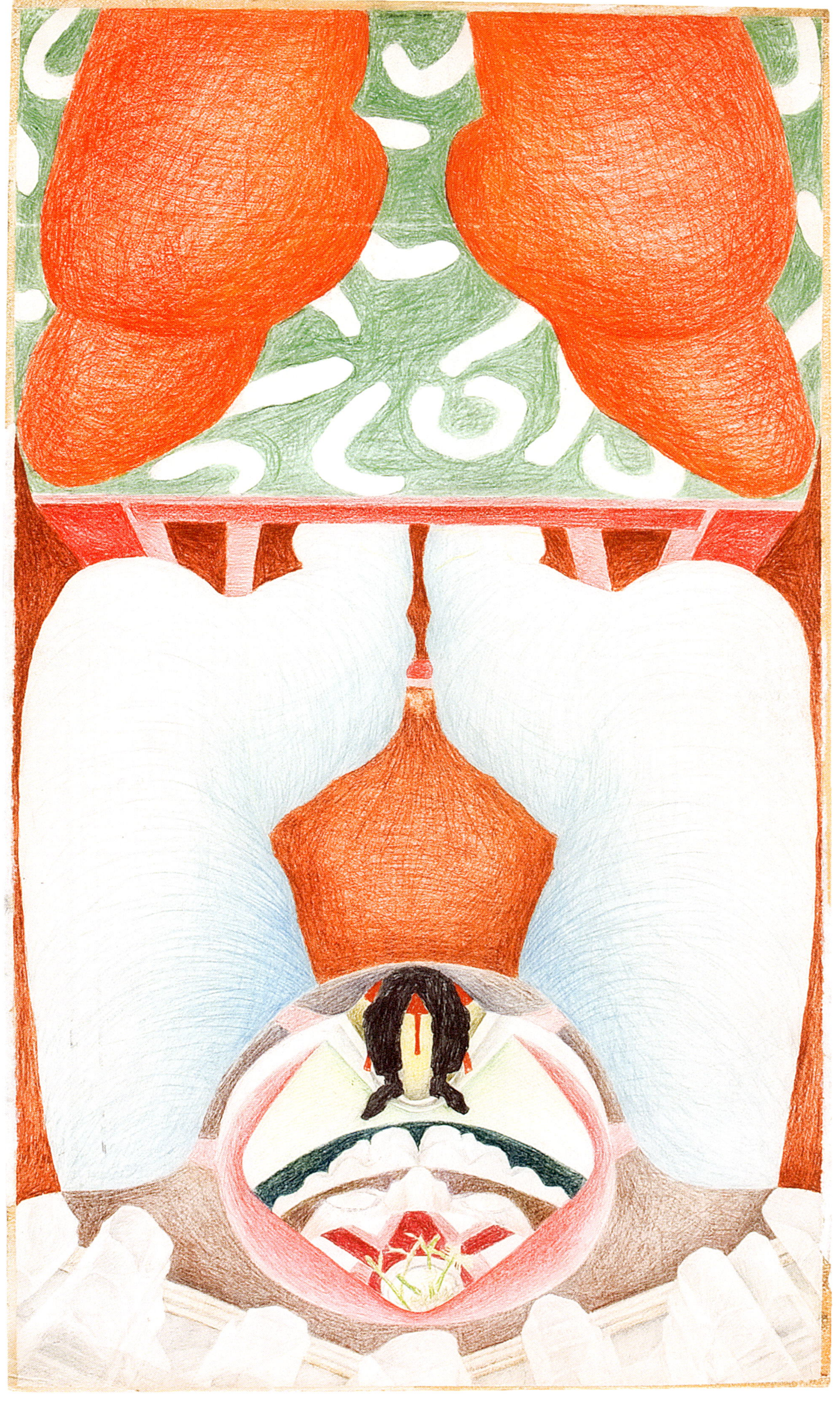

Untitled, ca. 1968
Mixed media on cardboard
31 × 23 ½ inches (78.5 × 60 cm)

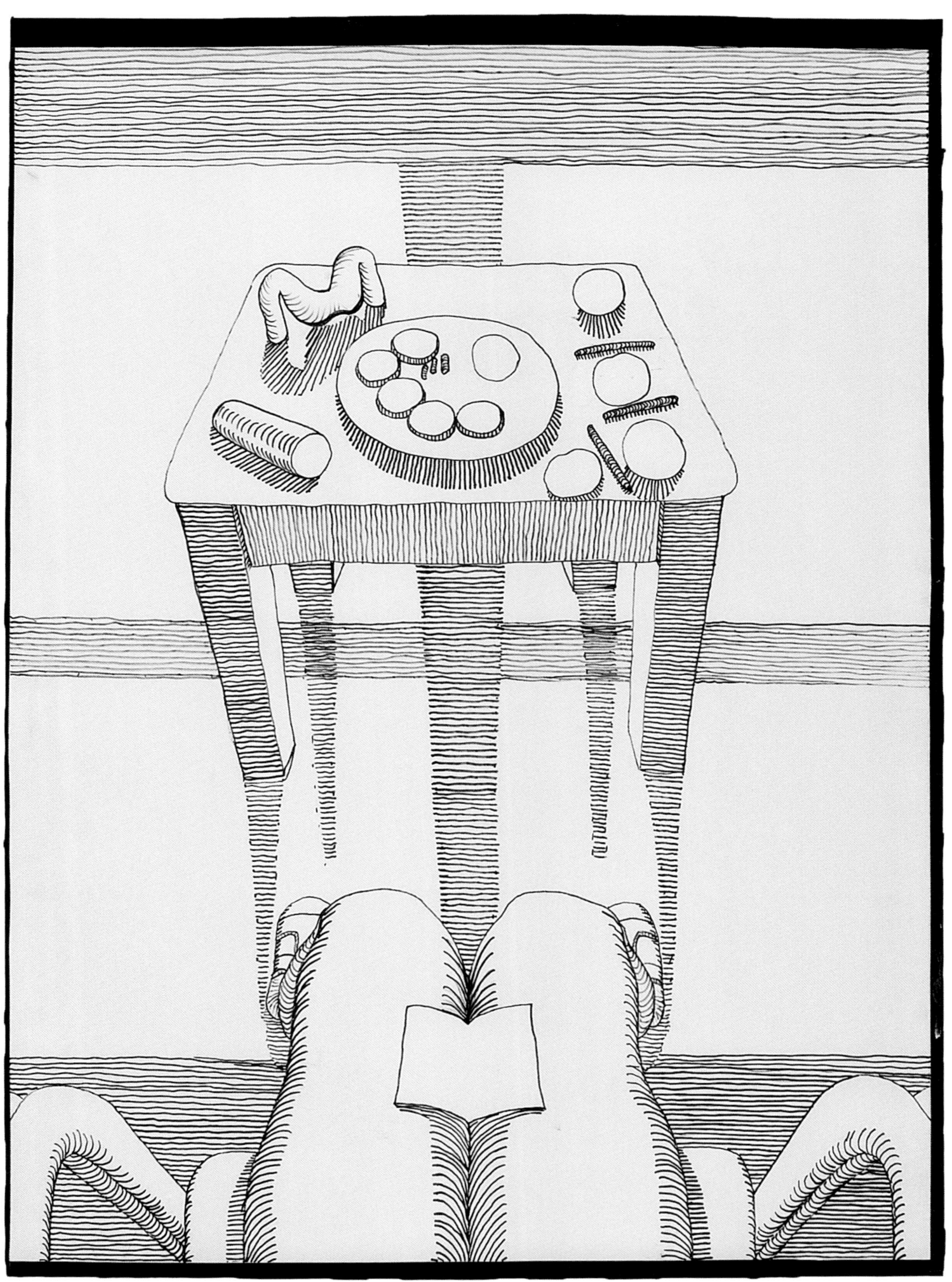

Untitled, before 1968
Mixed media on cardboard
22 × 20 inches (56 × 52 cm)

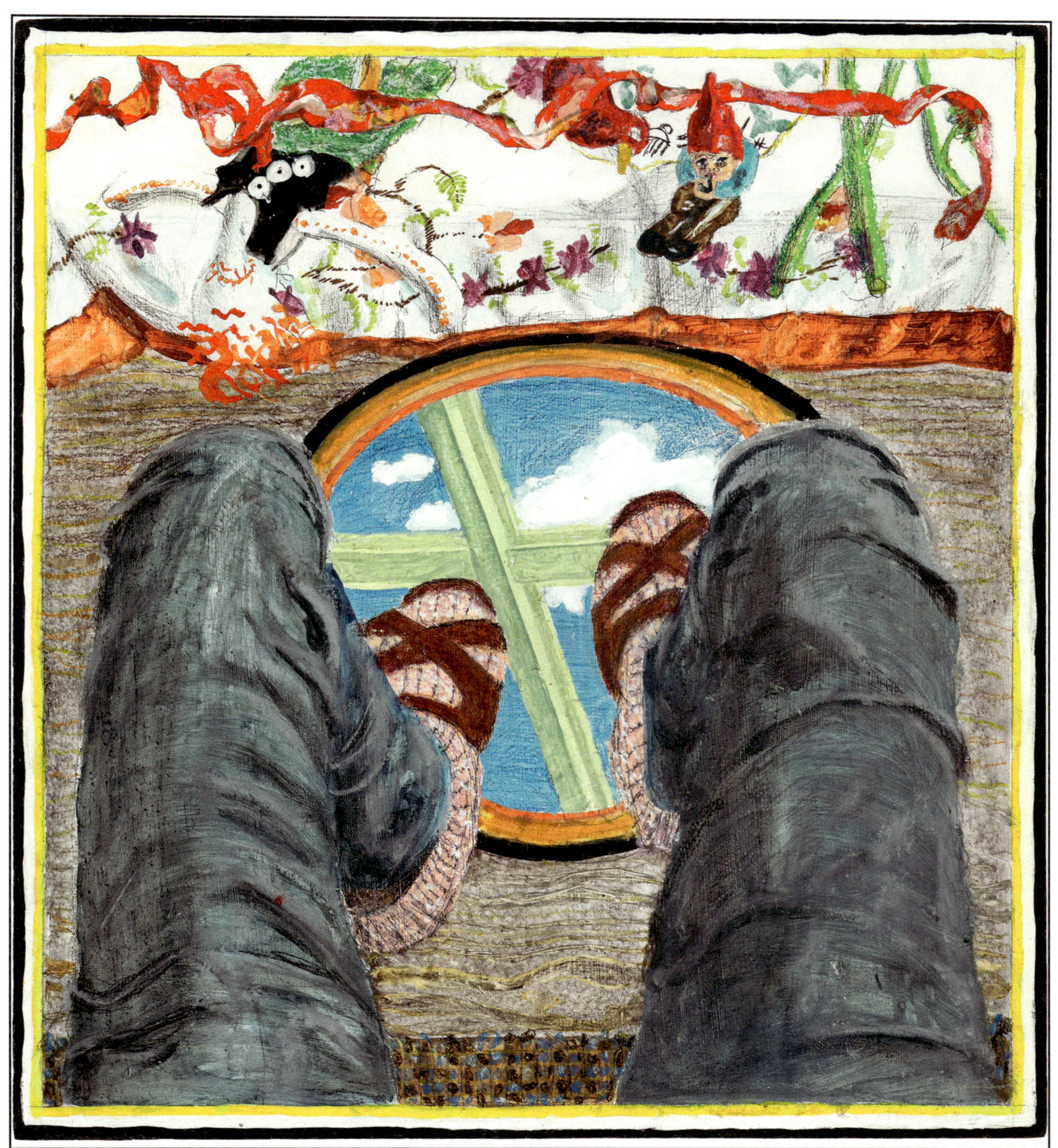

Table with round views, 1968
Mixed media on cardboard
78 ¾ × 39 ¼ inches (200 × 100 cm)

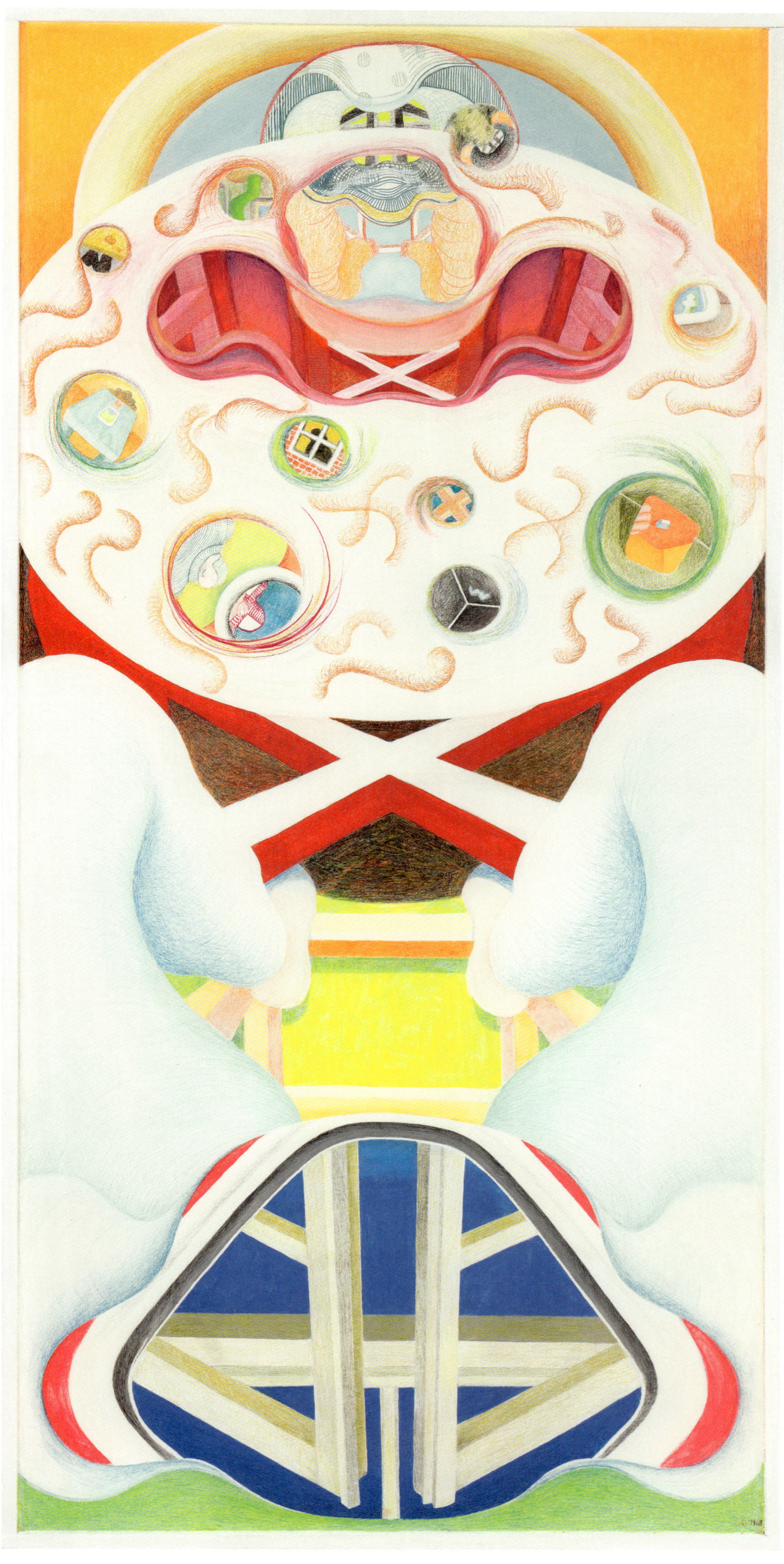

Being a Housewife, 1968/1973
Mixed media
Dimensions variable

Being a Housewife installation view at the Carpenter Center for the Visual Arts, 2019

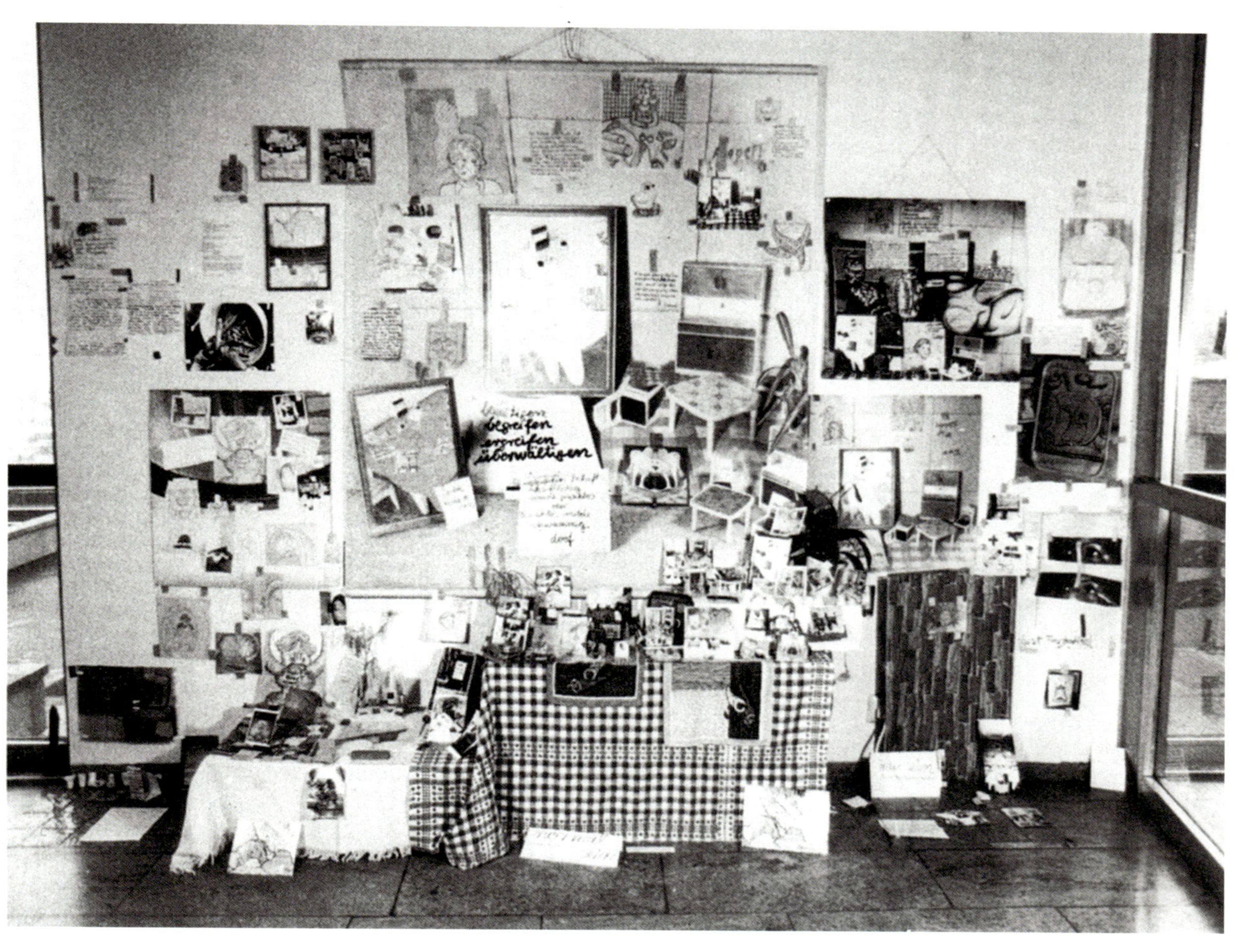
begreifen
ergreifen
überwältigen
doof

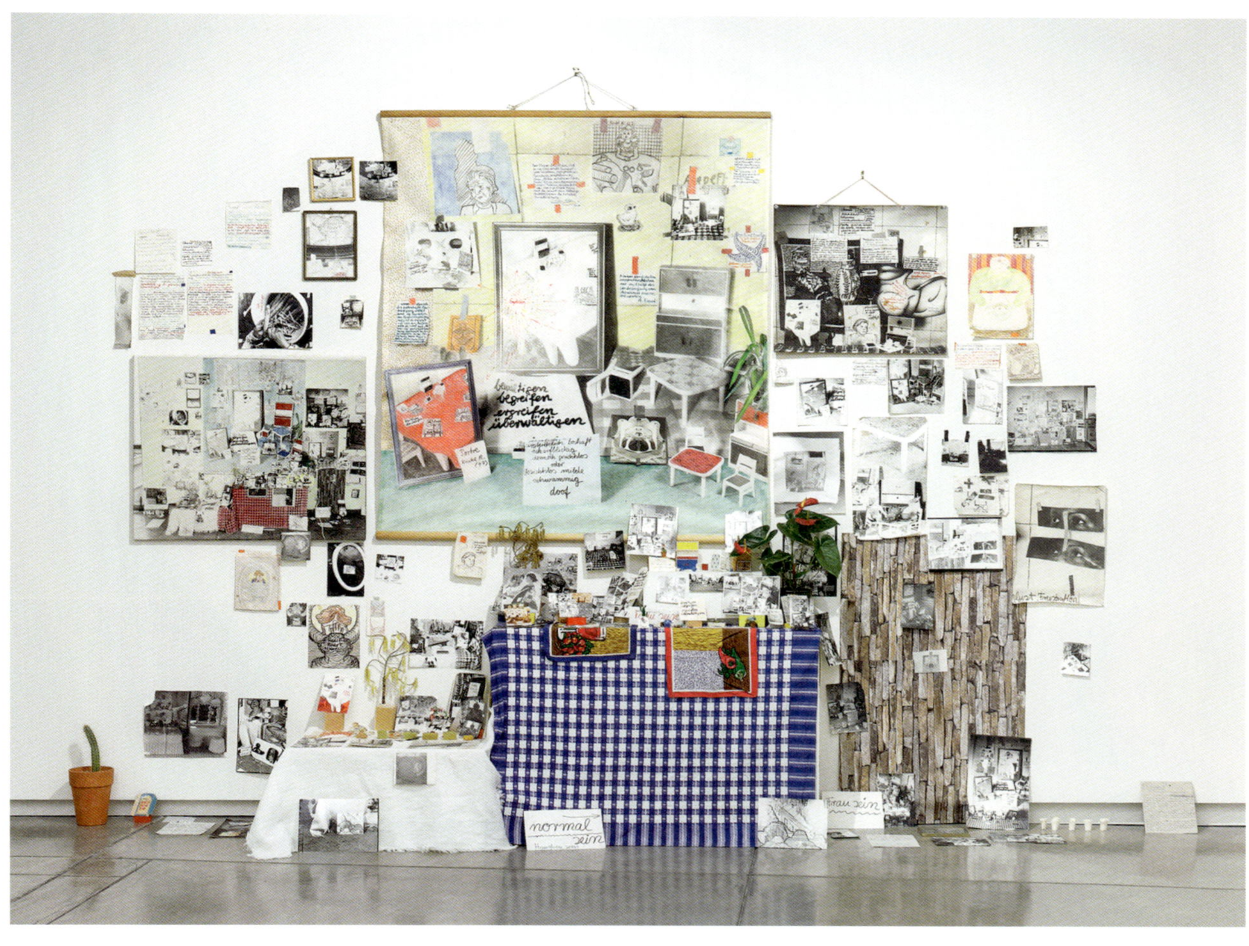
begreifen
ergreifen
überwältigen
doof
normal sein
Frau sein

Untitled, 1969/1970
Mixed technique on Masonite
59 × 48 inches (150 × 122 cm)

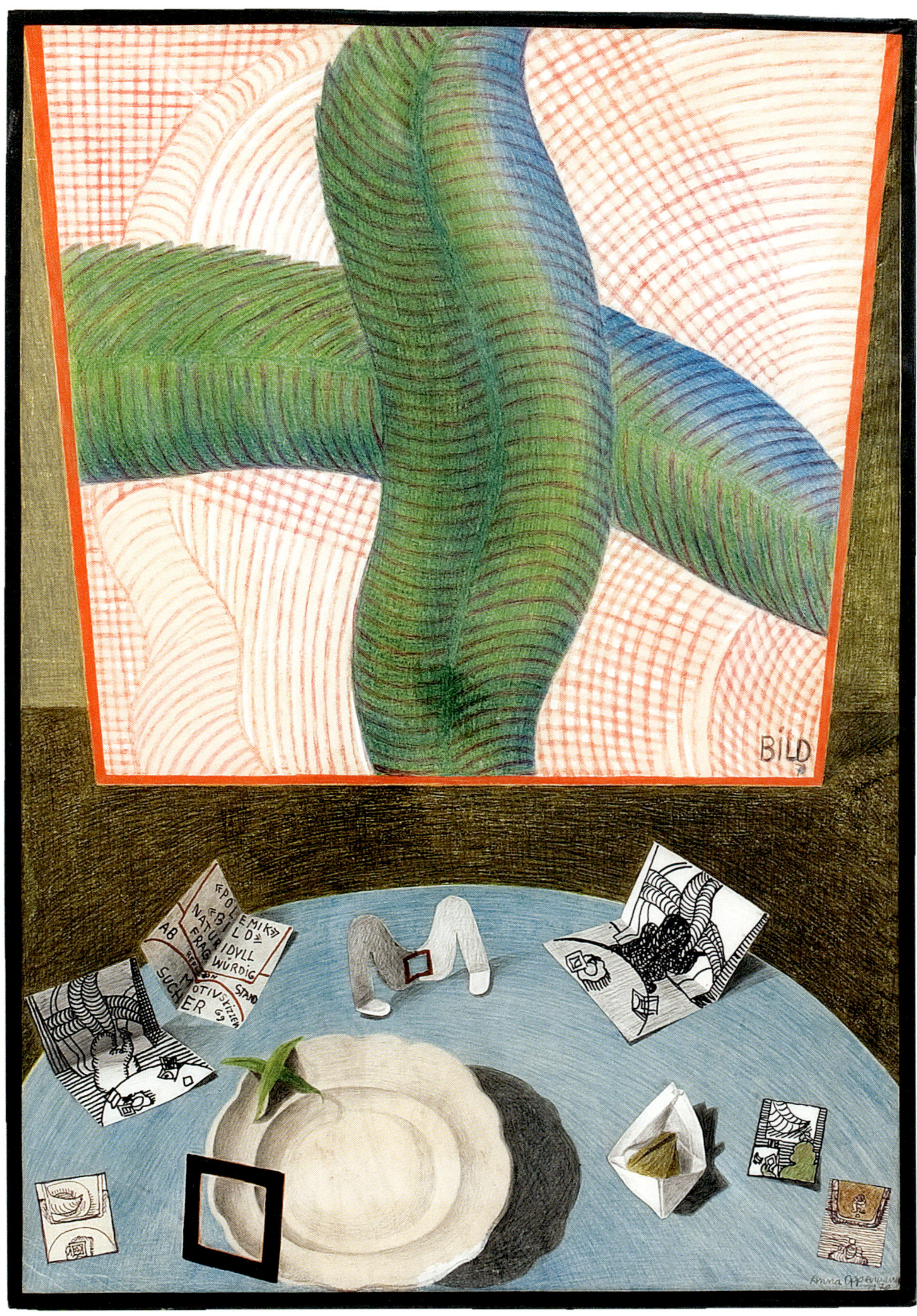

BILD
«POLEMIK»
«BILD»
NATURIDYLL
FRAGWÜRDIG
AB
STAND
MOTIVSKIZZEN
SUCHER

Untitled, ca. 1968
Mixed media on cardboard
33 × 19 ¾ inches (84 × 50 cm)

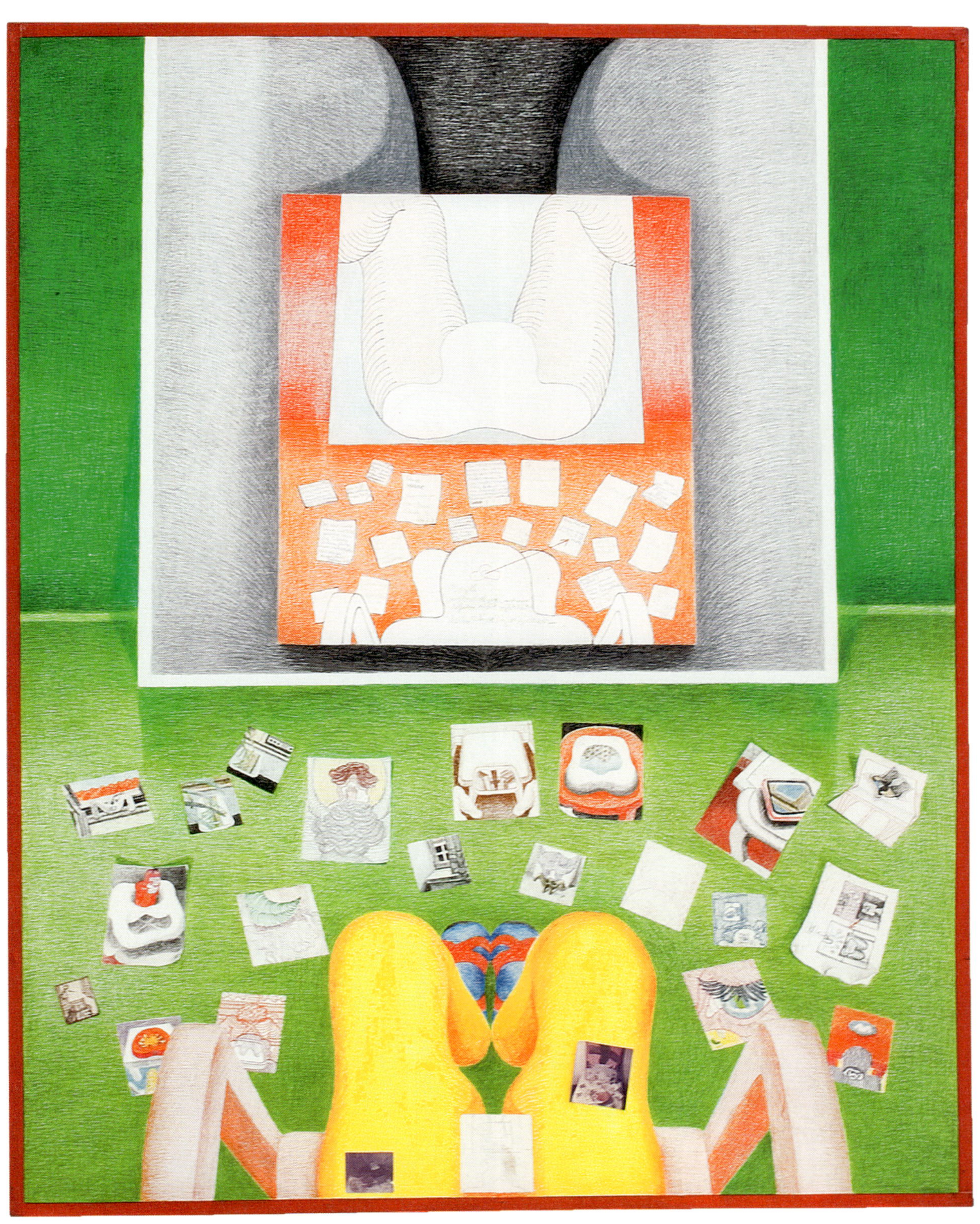

Indian girl, 1971
Colored pencil on Masonite
59 × 48 inches (150 × 122 cm)

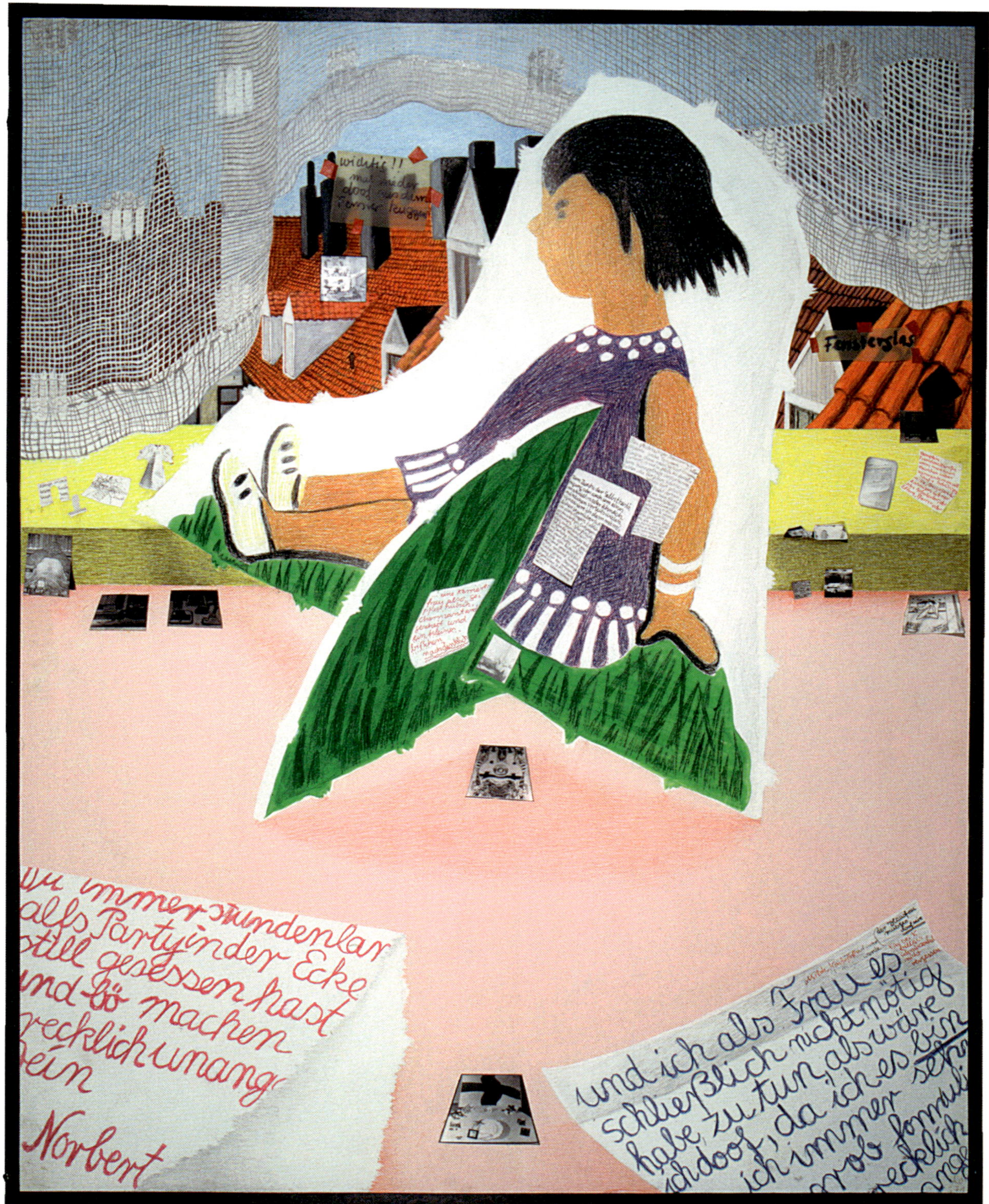
wichtig!!
Fensterglas
immer stundenlan
als Party in der Ecke
still gesessen hast
und bö machen
recklich unang
ein
Norbert
und ich als Frau es
schließlich nicht nötig
habe, zu tun, als wäre
ich doof, da ich es bin
ich immer sehr
grob formuli
recklich
ange

Untitled, ca. 1965/1968
Mixed media on Masonite
39 ¾ × 39 ¼ inches (101.3 × 100 cm)

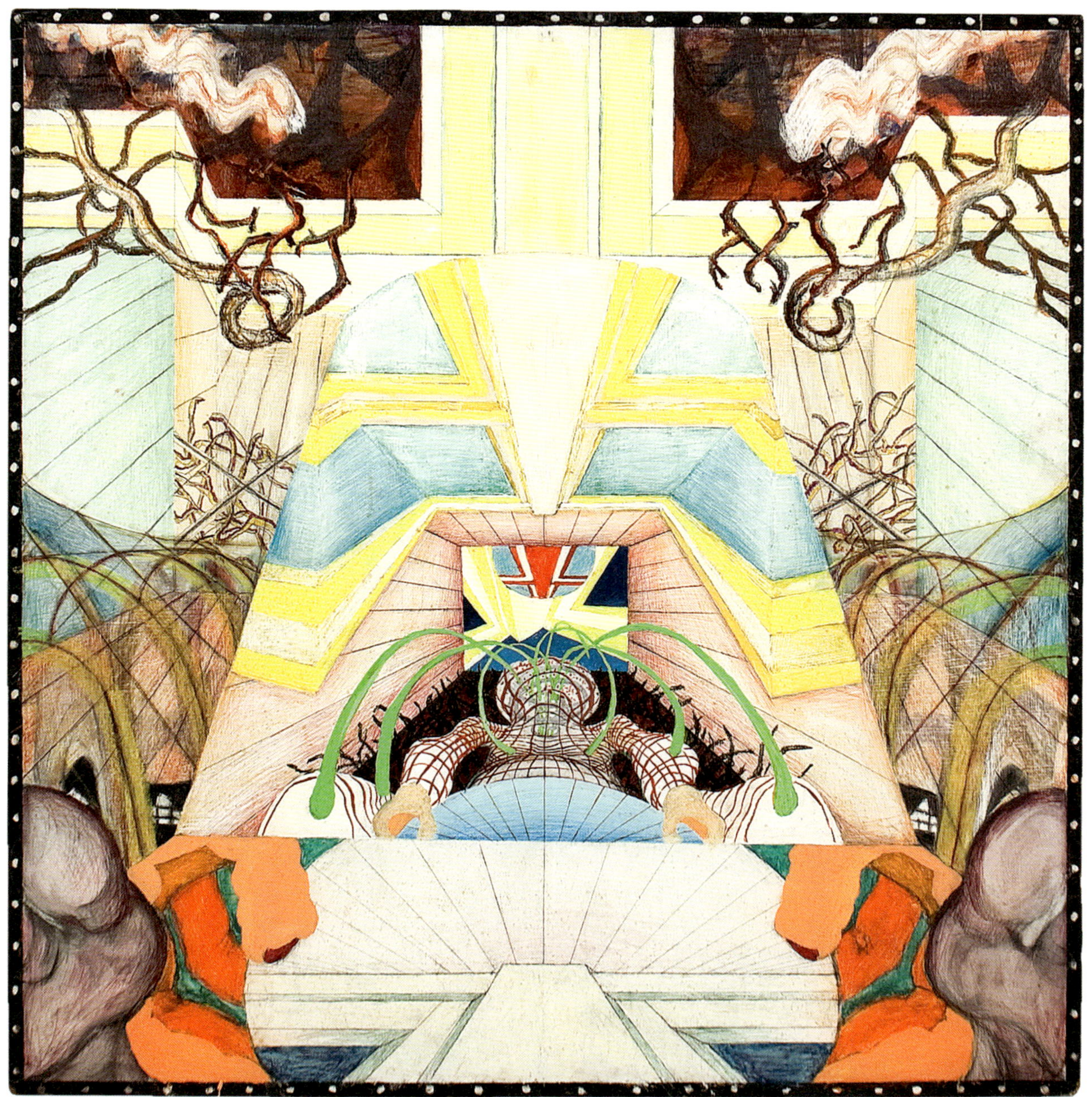

Untitled, ca. 1965/1968
Mixed media on Masonite
39 ½ × 39 ¼ inches (100.2 × 99.7 cm)

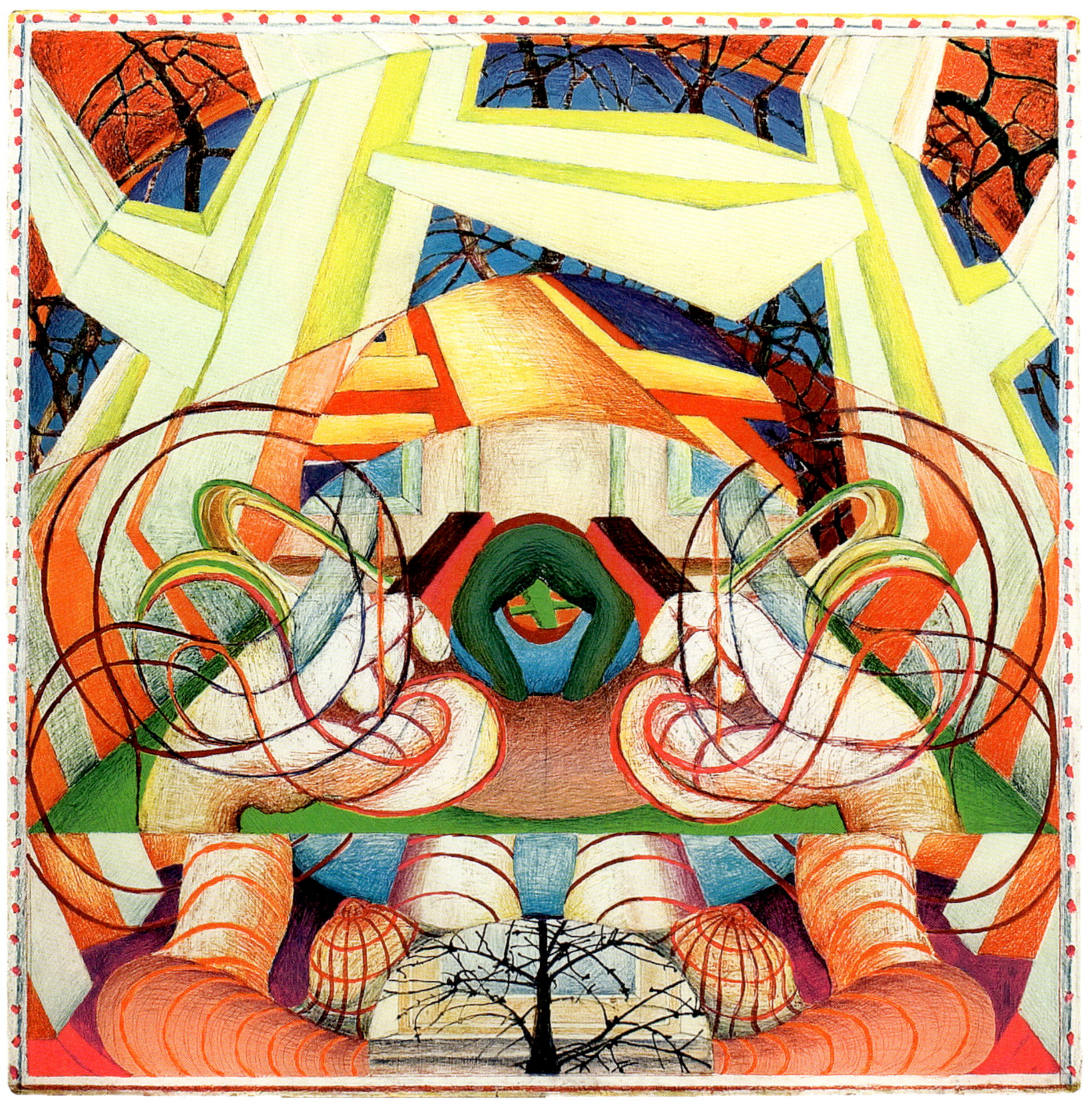

Untitled, ca. 1965/1968
Mixed media on Masonite
39 ¼ × 39 ¾ inches (100 × 101 cm)

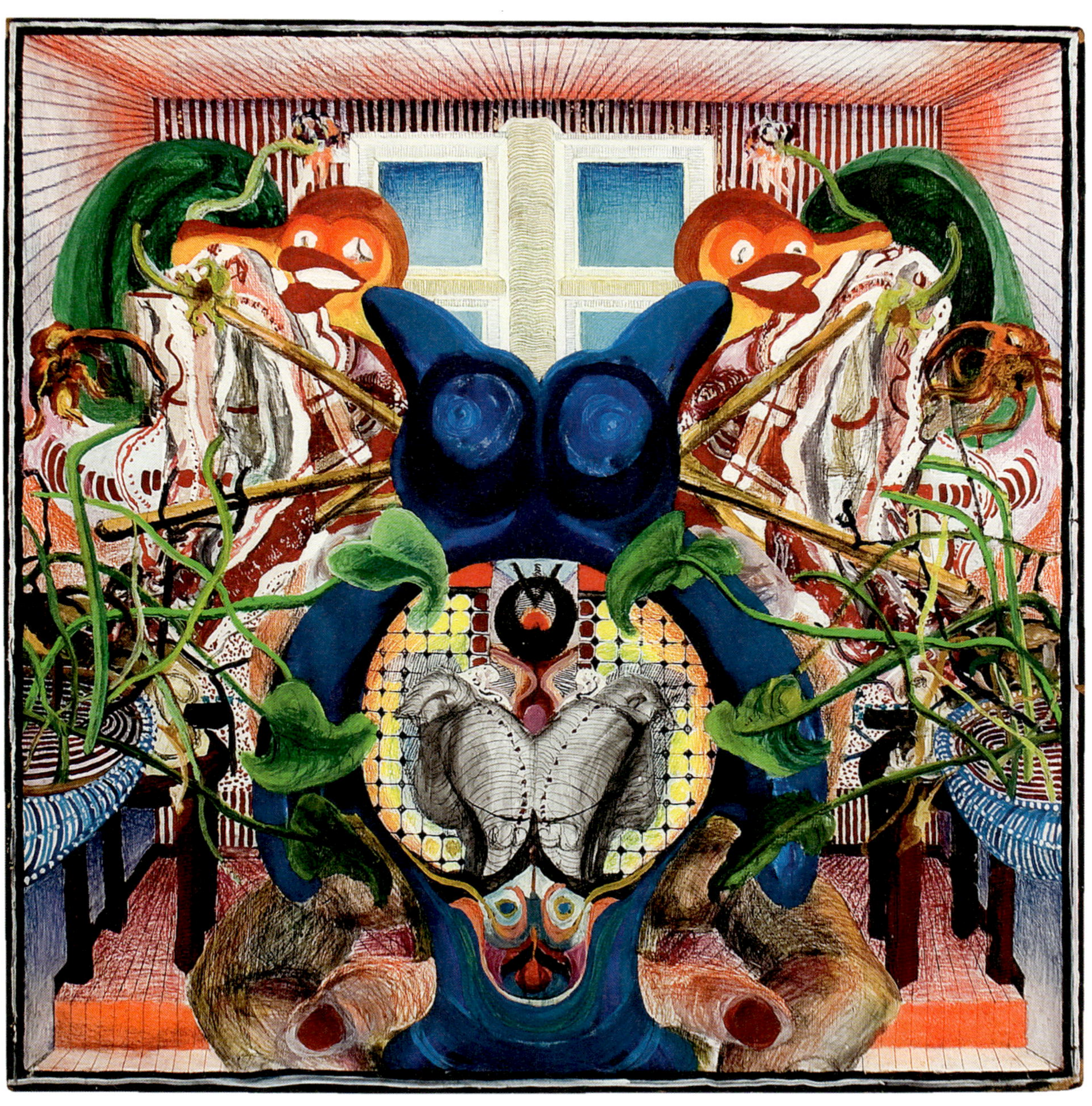

Untitled, ca. 1965/1968
Mixed media on Masonite
39 ¼ × 39 ¼ inches (100 × 100 cm)

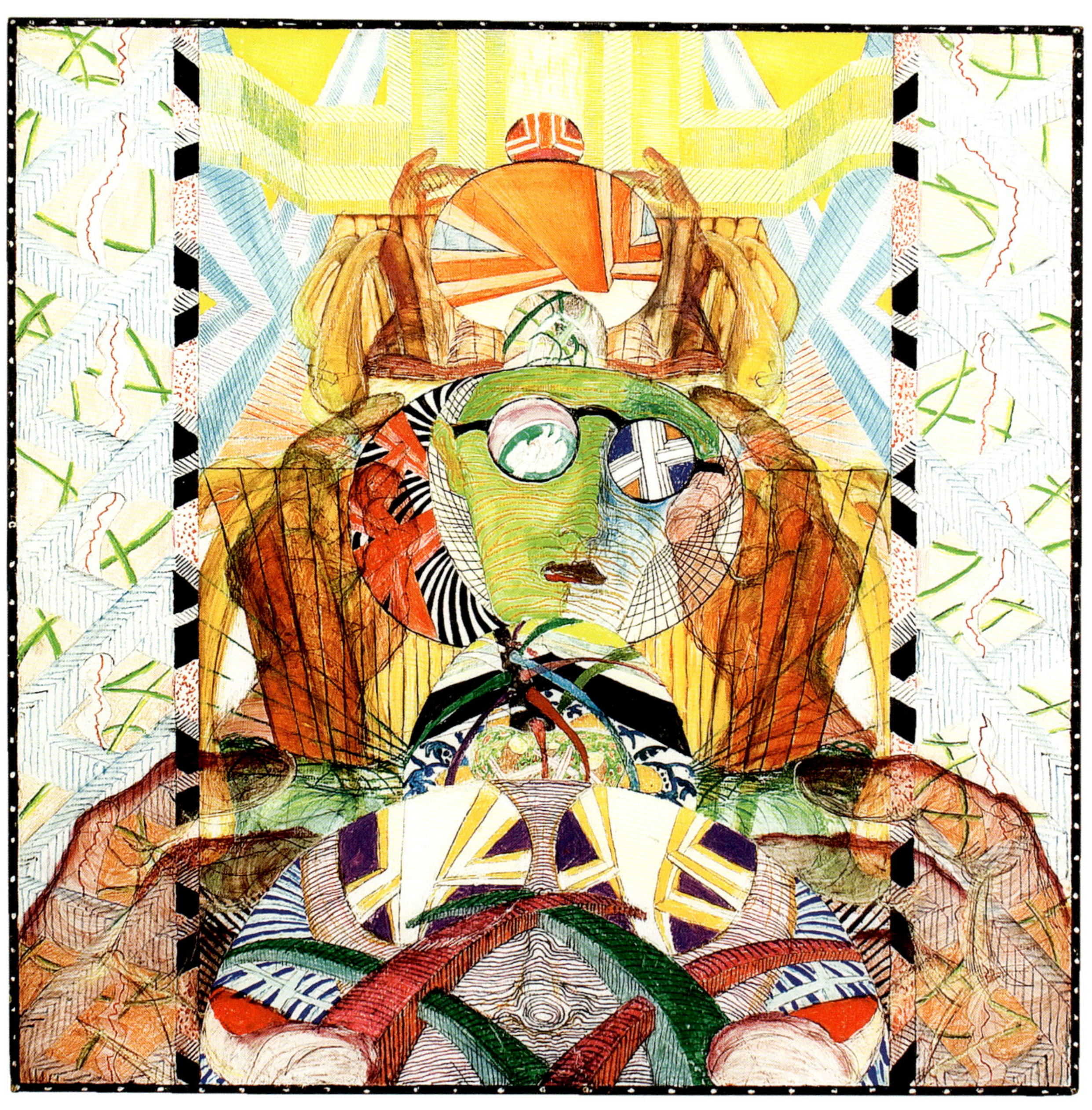

Untitled, ca. 1965/1968
Mixed media on Masonite
39 ¼ × 39 ¼ inches (100 × 100 cm)

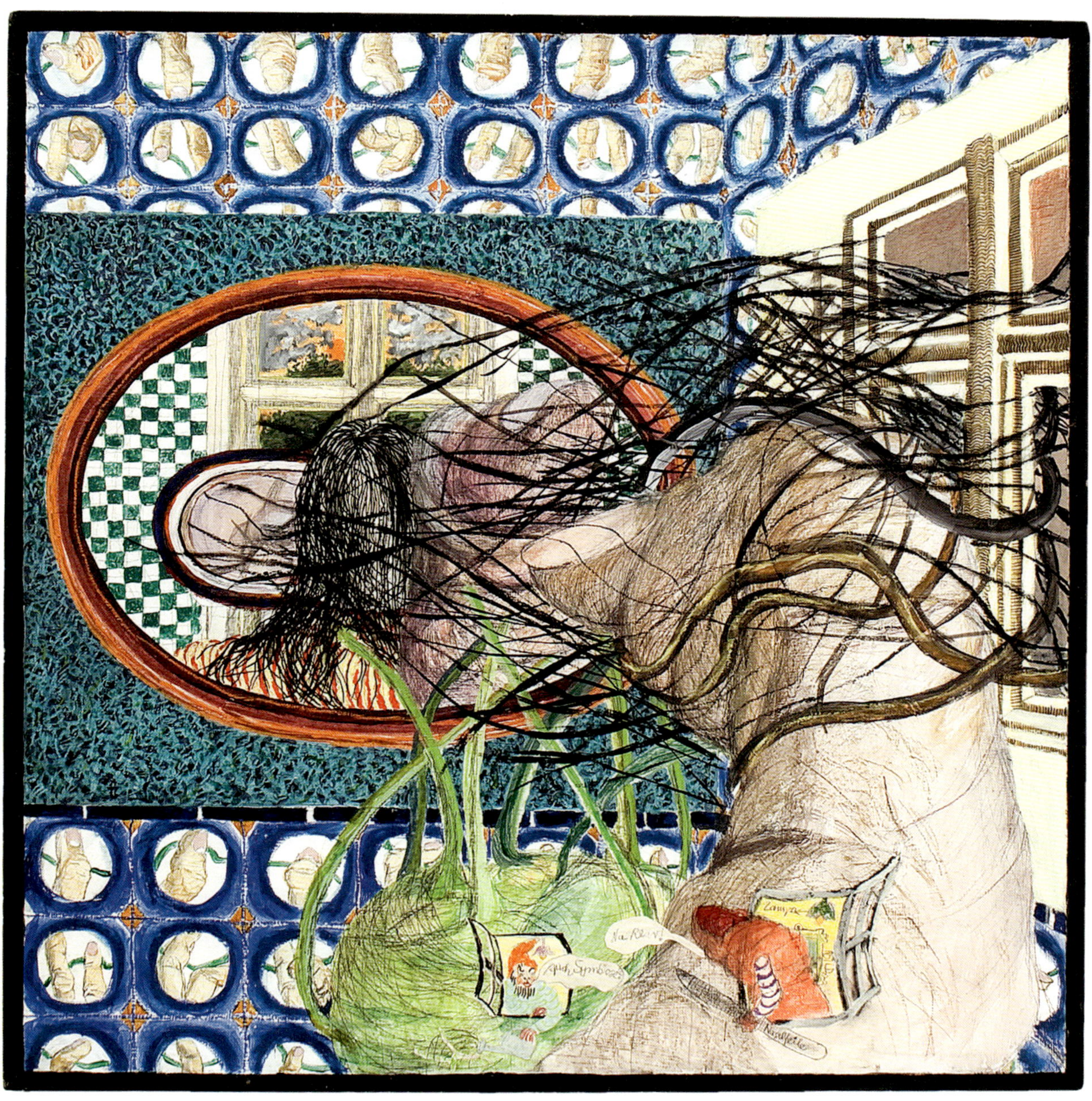

Untitled (Picture!), 1970
Lithograph
32 ¾ × 23 ¼ inches (83 × 59 cm)

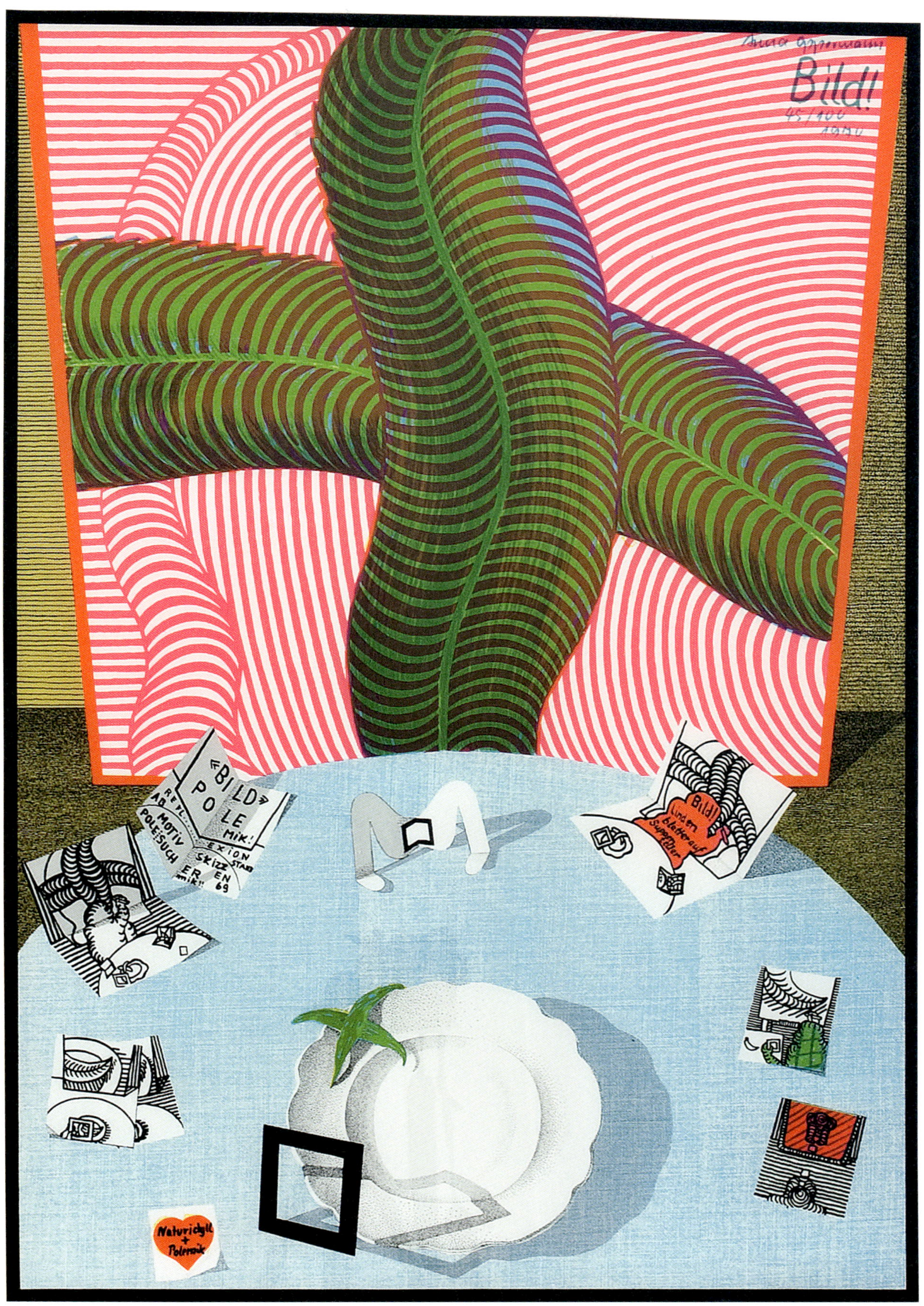
Bild!
45/100
«BILD»
PO LE
MIK!
MOTIV
POLEISUCH
Naturidyll
+
Polemik

Untitled, 1973
Lithograph
24 ¾ × 31 ½ inches framed
(63.2 × 80.2 cm)

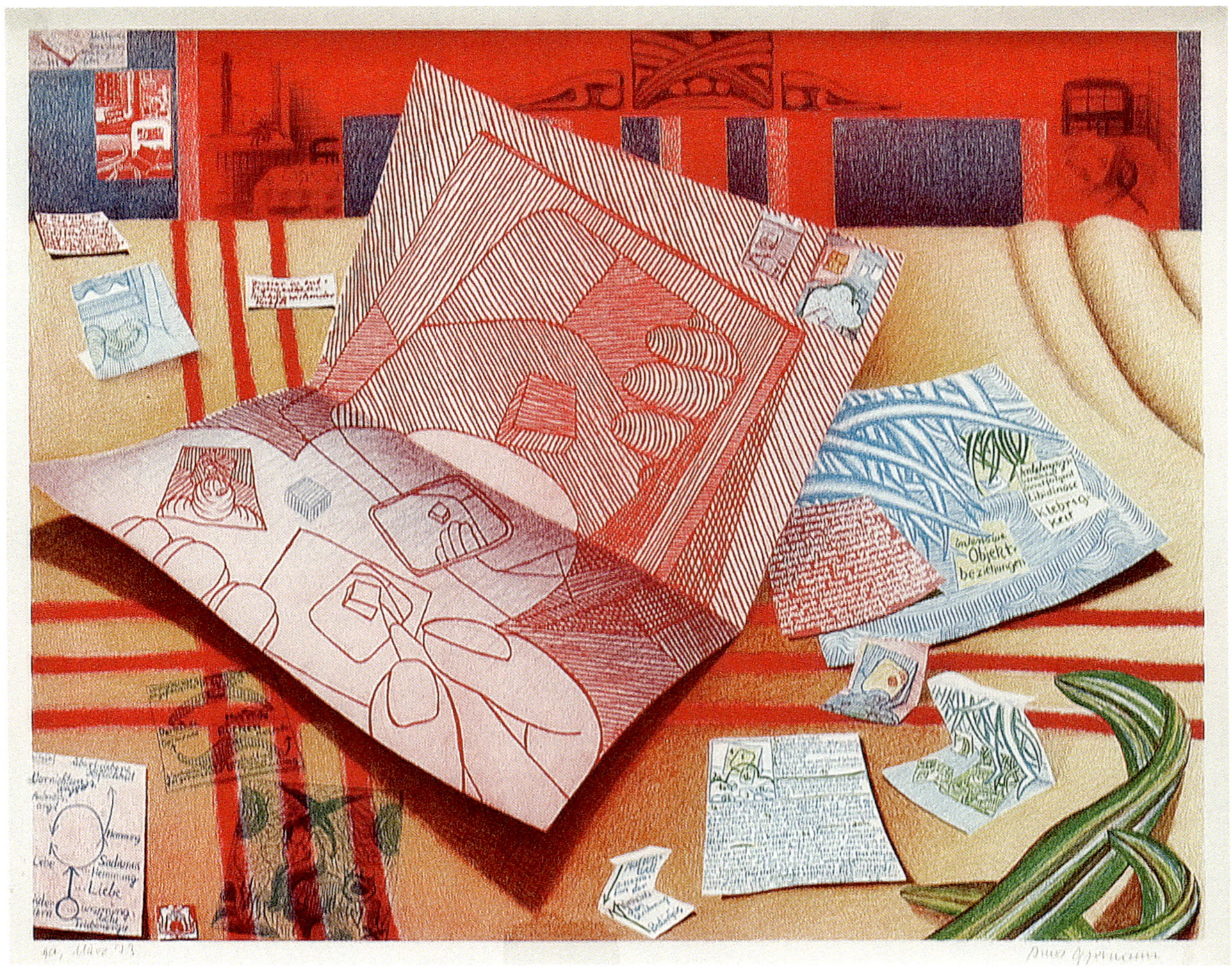

Lithography (Beans), 1974
Lithograph
22 × 30 inches (56.2 × 76.2 cm)

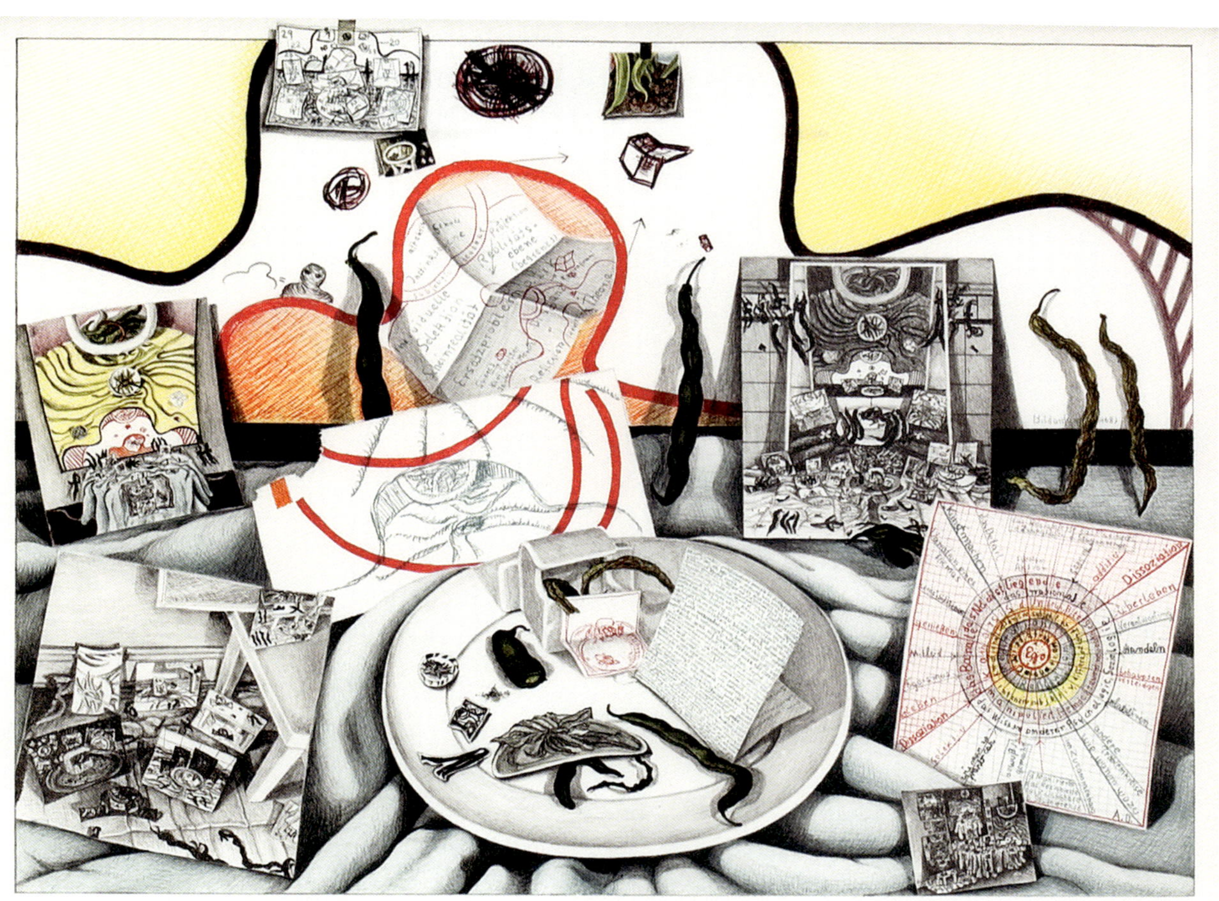
Dissoziation
Überleben
Handeln
Ego
Dissoziation

The closest thing, 1974
Lithograph
29 ¾ × 22 ¼ inches framed
(75.6 × 56.6 cm)

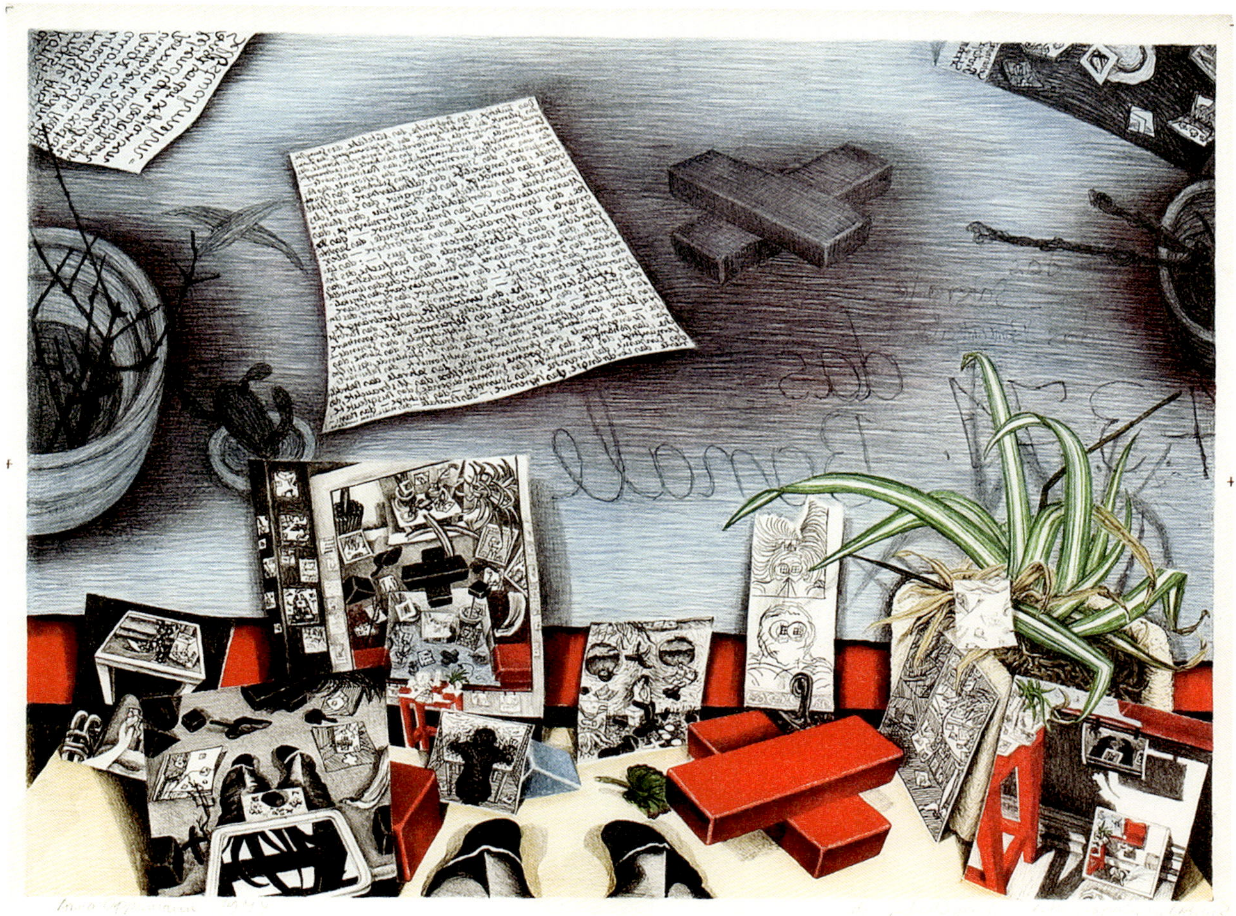

Explosion of a World Too Small: Anna Oppermann's Early Work

Dan Byers and Ute Vorkoeper

Ute Vokoeper wrote her dissertation on Anna Oppermann. While doing research toward the end of the artist's life, Vorkoper was engaged by Oppermann to help her install some of her final works. Vorkoeper has been restaging Oppermann's ensembles since her death in 1993. This conversation took place in the Sert Gallery of the Carpenter Center on June 20, 2019, the day before the opening reception for Anna Oppermann: Drawings.

DAN BYERS Shall we start at the beginning? Could you talk a little bit about what kind of training Anna Oppermann would have received in school, and how that might have influenced these early works?

UTE VORKOEPER In the beginning of her studies at the Hochschule für bildende Künste Hamburg [University of Fine Arts Hamburg, or HfbK], in 1962, it was mainly about painting and drawing. She started with an informal kind of painting-drawing, in which figurative elements were mixed in. These early works seem a little sleazy, deliberately unpleasant, and reminiscent of Art Brut. But they show that from the beginning she was interested in the human figure, and in figurative painting in general. Of course, later on she was also very influenced by Pop art, which evolved in parallel, and by artists who rediscovered figurative painting and then reinvented the image as a depiction of the world. HfbK has been and is still an important school in Germany, famous for conceptual art and a number of well-known graduates. But you have to realize that at the time Anna was studying, together with quite a few other female students, some of whom later became internationally known, such as Hanne Darboven and Rebecca Horn, there was not a single female professor or even a female teaching assistant at the HfbK. Only men.

DB Who were the specific artists that she was looking at in the 1960s? Did you ever talk to her about that?

UV No, unfortunately not. But one can see influences. Indispensable was the exchange with her husband, the artist Wolfgang Oppermann, whom she married in 1963. He was part of the Pop art movement in Germany and known in the 1960s for his comic-like figures which he printed on posters and also made into plastic cut outs. He taught and was the head of the printing department at HfbK. In her early pictures, Anna sometimes included elements of his works, as well as in her early ensembles that established her artistic reputation in the 1970s. One can trace how she reflected on Wolfgang's way of contouring figures and objects. During her time at the HfbK, she also met the German-American artist Richard Lindner and the British Pop artist Allen Jones, both of whom had been invited as guest professors. I think their influence is visible and perceptible—although Anna totally subverted the sexualization of the female body, for which both are known. Most of Anna's works on paper in the exhibition here were developed during that time or directly after her graduation.

By the way, Anna told Herbert Hossmann many times that Richard Lindner had told her to come to New York with him to start her career: in Hamburg he couldn't teach her anything more. Well, she didn't go to the United States. Never during her lifetime. I would say she had a whole bunch of very complex personal reasons for not doing it.

DB Was there anything else particular about Hamburg at the time that we might see in her work? Anything about material culture or place in particular?

UV I think what was most important in the development of her way of working was that she felt highly pressured to meet certain gender expectations. This had to do with the role of the woman in German society in the 1950s. It was the *Wirtschaftswunder* period after World War II, when Anna grew up, and it was a period of regression for women. During the final years of the war and just after, it was women who participated in the reconstruction of the country. There is a German term for them: *Trümmerfrauen* (women of ruins). They started to clear the destruction because there were no men around: they were war victims or prisoners of war. And then, five to ten years later, when the surviving men returned, the old structures began to reassert themselves. One-by-one the old paradigms were reinstalled, and stronger than before. This had to do with the strong need for normalization after losing the war, as well as with the offensive suppression of the crimes of the Third Reich. Women became simply housewives who could take care of happy families again. Their daughters felt this and started to rebel against the restrictive role. And of course, Anna Oppermann also had this problem. Particularly, since she was forced to live it herself—as the mother of a young son in the middle of the 1960s. She felt imprisoned at home and started to revolt against this situation within her art works. In her early works on paper, as well as in the early ensembles, she always fights against the notion of "being normal" (*Normal sein*), i.e. against social expectations and the damaging effects of social normalization. In my eyes this had a lot to do with the overall attempts to "normalize" German society after the Third Reich and the rejection of personal guilt for the past. The question of normalization followed Anna during her entire career.

DB I think one of the startling and surprising aspects of her work is the combination of these images of very traditional gender roles—housewives and aprons, etc.—in the middle of these extremely experimental, visually complex landscapes. Because when I think of other artworks that use similar colors or ways of drawing, the subjects they are picturing are also very experimental or non-normative. But here Oppermann is picturing these very traditional subjects and personae, in very mundane surroundings, but doing so with a deeply surreal approach which introduces the beautiful, bewildering tension in her work.

UV Yes, definitely. This results from her considerations of the ideal of the (male) artist, the question of what makes a genius, and of what qualities are ascribed to women: that they are naïve, or unable to have one's style (*Handschrift*) that is recognizable. She was always fighting against the notion of the genius and she reflected concepts of the male artist—mostly ironically—throughout her entire body of work. It was vital to her not to have one distinct mode or style. But in a way, of course, she ended up developing an absolutely different, non-individualistic, and non-genial—yet recognizable—style.

DB You've spoken before about how in certain works she's playing with different styles, quoting as it were, to telegraph a stereotyped "expressivity," or a kind of "dumb" mark-making that was overly decisive and authoritative.

UV Yes! This is what we see in the images that are surrounding us in the exhibition. You have chosen, for example, the painting over there: a mixture of "sleazy" painting and simple drawing. This piece is quite close to what she did in her very early works.

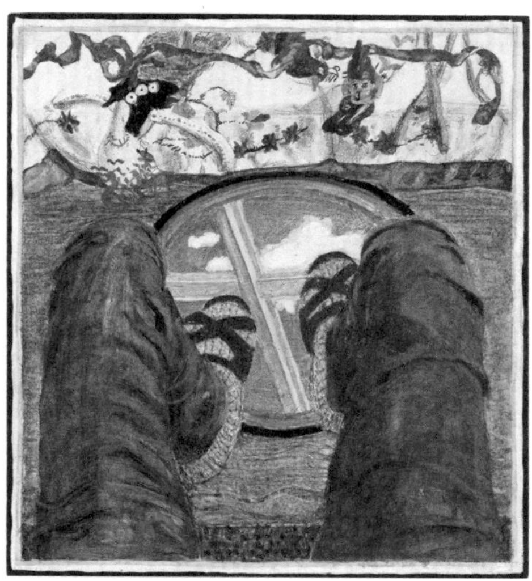

FIG. 1 *Untitled*, before 1968.

DB But she was using that style to reference those works rather than necessarily taking it up herself. She was self-aware …

UV Well, she was self-aware, but she did not reflect on styles in a merely self-reflexive or conceptual way. The references to art theory, other artists, and all kinds of different styles in her work occur out of the felt necessity to depict the world, i.e. all for her important aspects of world in more than one perspective. By using different styles, she wanted to expand her own view and to integrate the perception of other. That her work is not "conceptual" but an attempt to develop a new method of presentation and representation at the same time: *this* is the reason why I have remained engaged with it for so many years.

Each image in this exhibition is a condensed metaphor. You can read it. One *should* read it. Once, after discussing her ensemble method, for which she became famous, Anna suddenly asked me:

"What do you see in the images within the ensembles? Did you ever try to look at them closely? Did you try to read them?" I was bewildered. I had to admit that I never looked at what they depict seriously enough. This changed my view. Whereas the early paintings and drawings on exhibit here are still distinct works, the later ensembles are arrangements of countless images. You can see this in the early ensemble *Being a Housewife*. However, Anna considered the images within the ensembles also as "readable," some more, some less, but always interpretable like allegories. They can be conceived as chapters: condensed aspects of the topic with which the ensemble is dealing. You can read them image by image, chapter by chapter. This shows once more that she was never interested in mere formal or conceptual investigations. There was always a narrative, or parable almost, motivating that formal and conceptual play.

DB Perhaps we should read one now?

UV It is not that we have to discover one single intention. The works aim for an open and endless form of reading. While trying to decipher you always have to add your own interpretation since there are so many gaps, layers, and overlaps. Each picture opens up a heteronomous field of thinking by itself and thereby produces an even wider field of interpretation. And each new picture widens this field again, shifts and spreads meaning.

DB Speaking of images being read, how do you think the actual text—handwriting—came into her work?

UV Well, she herself mentioned a situation where she had chosen an object, made a drawing and noted a description and laid it all out in front of her on a table. She could no longer decide which element was more valuable, and which was more telling about the object and its context. So, she decided that all parts should have the same importance and should be combined. And look, here we see an early, powerful example of this artistic thinking demonstrated in this stunning picture with the cigarette.

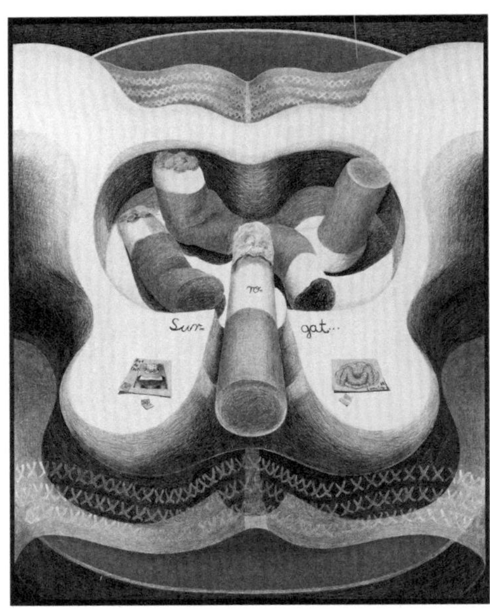

FIG. 2 *Antidesign*, 1970–1972.

The image itself is pretty clear: a large ashtray provides a metaphor for a female belly and a burning cigarette that looks like a phallus is penetrating it. The little word *Surrogat* (surrogate), which is written on the ashtray, manifests the pain of this allegorical penetration, but it also points to a theoretical—more distant—reflection of the situation. It reads like a sudden insight that opens up new layers of meaning. This reflection from a distance offers a way out of the purely physical experience.

DB The symbolism is not subtle, and yet so many visceral symbols sit so close to each other that "easy" reading becomes difficult. The rather abject forms are also rendered with great seductive power. This is partially due to the extreme perspective she used. The cigarette is both jutting out, toward us, but this also opens up the picture, creating a kind of deep space for us to imagine ourselves in. What about this large, tall work—isn't it from the mid 1960s?

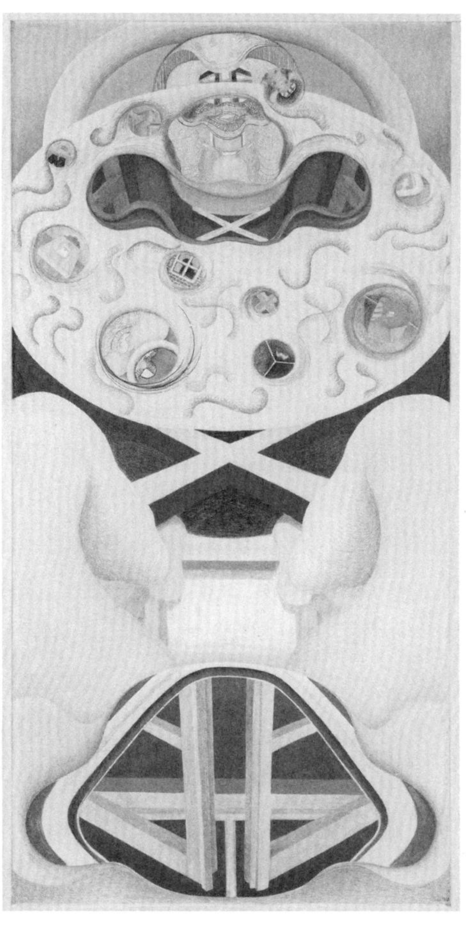

FIG. 3 *Table with round views*, 1968.

UV Unfortunately, but very fittingly, Anna rarely dated and signed her works. I guess that she realized already in the midst of the 1960s that she had problems with finished works. The most important period of Anna's artistic development was from the mid-1960s to 1972. During that time, she always switched between producing single paintings and gradually developing her ensemble method. But even though she had already started to create small ensembles in her kitchen, in the end she still decided to exhibit paintings in her first solo exhibition in 1968–69. Well, I think, she saw herself mostly as a graphic artist until that time. She showed a series of pictures, including this one that we're looking at right now. These very condensed and focused psychedelic pictures originate from her last years of study. At that time, she had already begun for some years to open up the perspectives by adding drawings, photographs, and texts. Not until 1972 did she take the next important step: to quit the single picture and instead fragment it into many pieces that were shown ensemble or, in English, together.

DB I think this is an important point, in terms of the reciprocity between her ways of working, that she was making early ensembles while she was still making the large-scale drawings. Perhaps this is one reason why the cut-out photographs of other drawings make their way onto the surface of her major drawings. She must have been photographing her works, and cutting them out, for experimentation in her ensembles as well?

UV It seems like that, and it makes it sometimes difficult to decipher all the elements of a picture. With the knowledge of her later work, it is easier to understand what she wanted to indicate with certain photographic references. We can also interpret this as an important moment in her working method: it was an interplay of opening up and closing again. It's about frames, about being framed, shifting the frame, and thereby creating new frames. In her ensemble *Being an Artist*, which is one of her largest works, the frame itself is a central motif. She cut frames from paper or used empty slide frames to point to the infinite number of images that can be produced. She called these frames *Bildsucher*, or viewfinder, to find …

DB … An infinity.

UV *Unendlich viele Bilder*: infinitely many pictures, as she noted in *Being an Artist*.

DB This aspect of her work makes me ask how aware—or how interested—she was in the idea of reproducible images and image culture of the '60s (or of the twentieth century, for that matter). She's obviously photographing and assembling photographs, and thinking through images, but did the idea of idea of an endless image culture, or the weight of the photo archive engage her thinking? Did these ideas enter into her interest in Pop?

UV Well, I think she was aware of that. But it was not the question of reproduction itself that interested her. In fact, she used reproductive techniques to fix singular ephemeral scenes and to generate singular and quite auratic and somehow enigmatic images. This is really special. There are infinite shifts of view, but not in order to create series.

DB It's all different perspectives on the same image.

UV She used photography to combine different time layers and thereby create an inherently fragmented and endless image of things which were meaningful to her. She developed a fractal image, so to speak, that shows its objects from various perspectives and with many overlaps but, at the same time, allows for future changes.

DB And it's always different. The quality of the difference or the shift becoming a vital space.

UV Right! With every shift of frame, she could reopen what she had fixed before. And she not only shifted the frame but also all the particles that were inside the frame. She rearranged her arrangements. This openness allowed her resets, modifications, and all kind of additions.

DB It seems like very rarely was the image of just one thing. It's always an image of multiple objects in complex, often confusing, "conversation." So, it's not a decisive image. Nor is it Andy Warhol with an icon. And then within that complexity, you have all these different angles and all these different worlds because we're standing in the gallery of twelve works and the world that each one depicts is highly limited, tiny. The world exists, say, at her table, in her lap. It's in her head. It's in her ashtray. It's at the desk. Yet there are so many relationships, worlds, and sets of symbolic dialogues condensed into these highly limited spaces, where her body meets furniture, or quotidian objects just sitting there.

UV As I said before, this is what she felt like at that time: imprisoned in the tiny world of the housewife. Fittingly, the all-over repeated check pattern of curtains and tablecloths in her early images remind me of prison bars. And she started her artistic reflections with things that entered this tiny world. Also, her considerations about being an artist, the dealing with nature or drawing from nature—from plants, which was really important for her—started with things that came to her, that encountered her. Then she discovered, as she noted later, the mirror as a tool not only to reflect herself or the world, but to expand this prison; to fragment it and to widen the narrow horizon by multiplying the perspectives. This was her way of revolting against gender roles and narrowness. Her revolution. I think this way of dealing with settings is in a way post-structuralist—even though Anna did not really examine poststructuralism herself. Nevertheless, she deconstructed in a very singular—not theoretical, but visual—way these everyday conventions which appeared to be absolutely fixed. And she did not stop at that point, but fragmented and rearranged the fragments again and again.

With some distance, we can see a change of interests within Anna's work throughout the years. The tiny world of the 1950s and '60s no longer occupied her by the 1980s. She moved toward more philosophical aspects of making art in the "postmodern" world. This change from private and specific interests to more political and general topics, she stated as central to her way of working. It is inherent in every ensemble as well, as it characterizes the development of her whole oeuvre. Thereby, the mirror remained one of her central tools until her late large work *Paradoxical Intentions*. This work is intensively multicolored, reminiscent of the early pictures we see here in Cambridge. But it is also an ensemble, dealing with death, disease, and with the reflection of her working method, with illusion and shine (*Schein*), with lies and truth.

DB It strikes me that among all of these mirrors, there's no image of her face. I know that she made other work that was very much about her face, and a series of photographic self-portraits. But in the drawings, her presence as described by a recognizable face is never present. And it's only her silhouette, or the absence of her body, that somehow finds its way into the mirror.

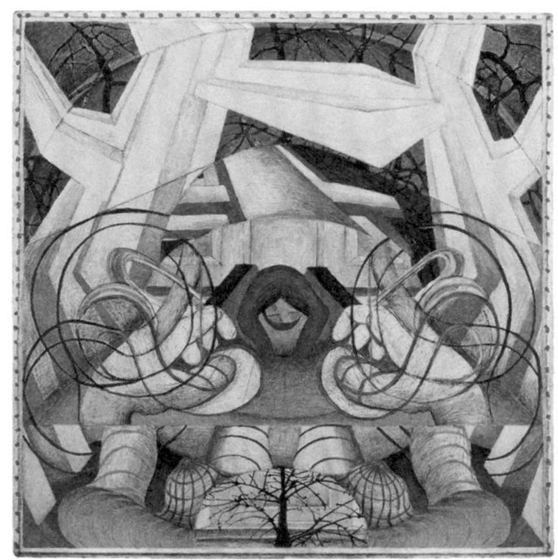

FIG. 4 *Untitled*, 1965–75.

UV Anna's face is mostly an absent or invisible part of her body. In her large and important ensemble *Being Different*, she appears all over but always hidden behind her hair. She is visible, but not recognizable. The work which you mention—the large series of staged self-portraits from the 1960s and early 1970s—she never exhibited during her lifetime. But also, these images do not show her actual self. Instead, they show the artist hiding behind her own stereotype frozen face as if behind a mask while being looked at by an anonymous viewer. She used a camera with a self-timer.

DB I didn't realize that!

UV Take this woman, for example. It's not Anna, it's somebody else. Like a projection of her. But all these knees …

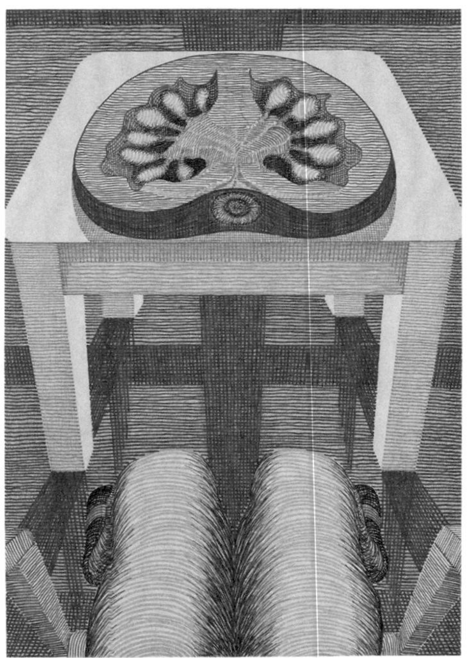

FIG. 5 *Untitled*, 1970.

DB Those were her, but then there's this, this figure is an archetype. And what does this text say?

UV "1970 housewife B."
"Age 47"
"after cleaning the dishes sitting at the kitchen table."
And there is a list noting "Milch, Eier, Klopapier, Margarine." It's a …

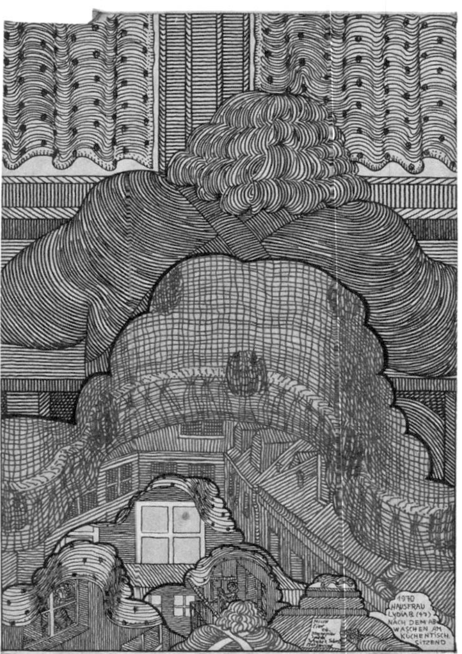

FIG. 6 *Untitled*, ca. 1968/1970.

DB … a shopping list.

UV And nearly the same shopping list you can find in *Being a Housewife*.

DB It's interesting to think about the writing in her work, which is very philosophical and about the nature of being, next to this writing, which is very functional and banal, with the two modes of writing existing on the same level.

UV After her death it was sometimes very difficult to decide what was part of the work and what was simply private. But in that case, the shopping list is a really important element of the housewife ensemble. It has a meaning in this context. Moreover, the switch between high and low was another important aspect of her working method. Just as she rejected a single handwriting, she tried to integrate different levels of access into her pictorial dialogues. So, she linked quotations from philosophy, psychoanalysis, and literature with text fragments from newspapers and magazines, as well as with analytical, colloquial, sometimes very ironic, commentary.

DB Turning from the three drawings that feature versions of this housewife archetype, I want to look at these drawings that are clearly drawn from Oppermann's own perspective; including her own body in the drawing. So many of her works put us inside of her head, not just in her inner world, but looking out, seeing her surroundings as she would, somehow very clear-eyed and fantastical at the same time.

UV She tried to create perspectives that pull the viewer into the viewing position that she herself took while drawing. Anna stated once that she had imagined that the

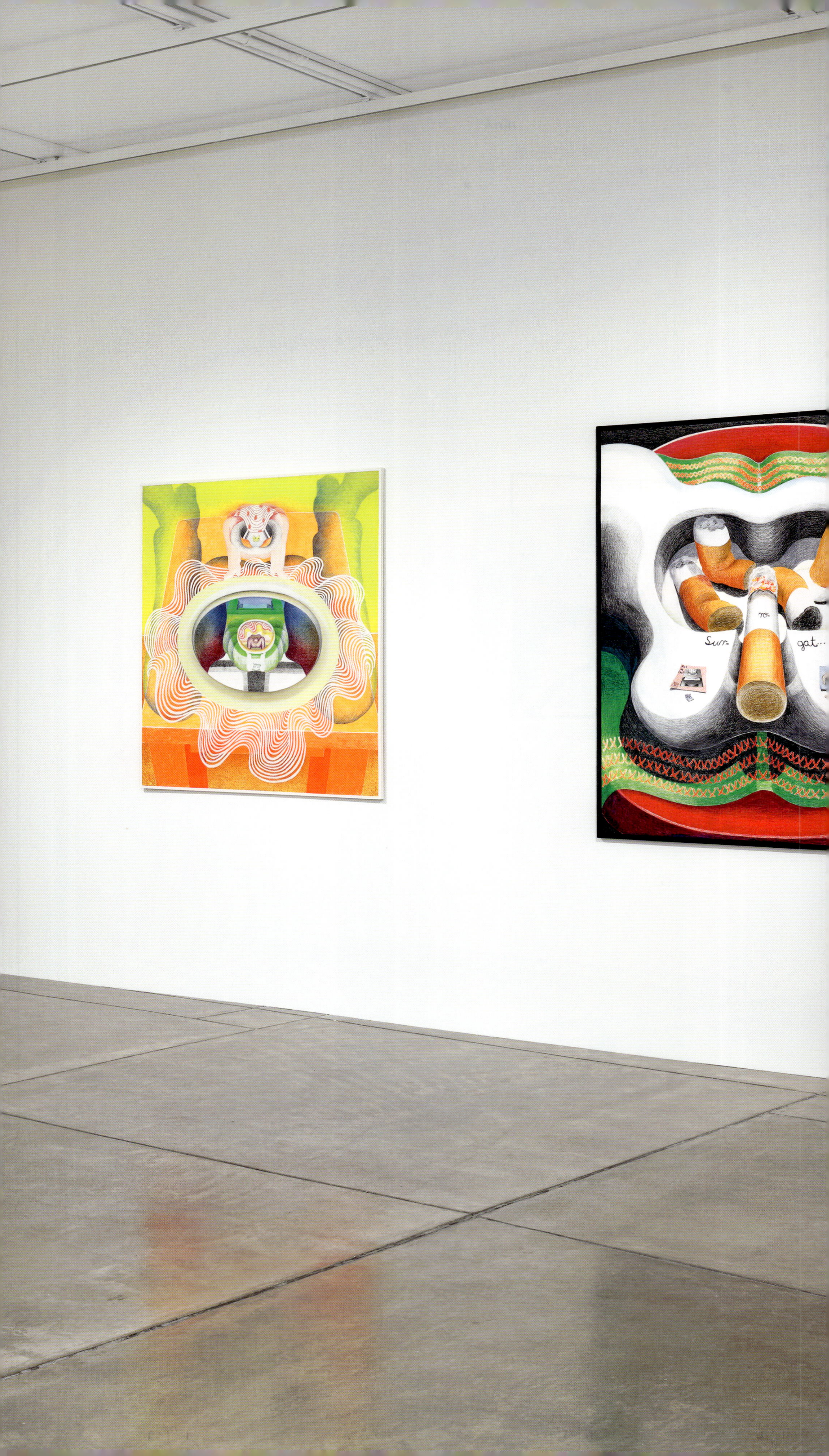
Sur=
ro=
gat...

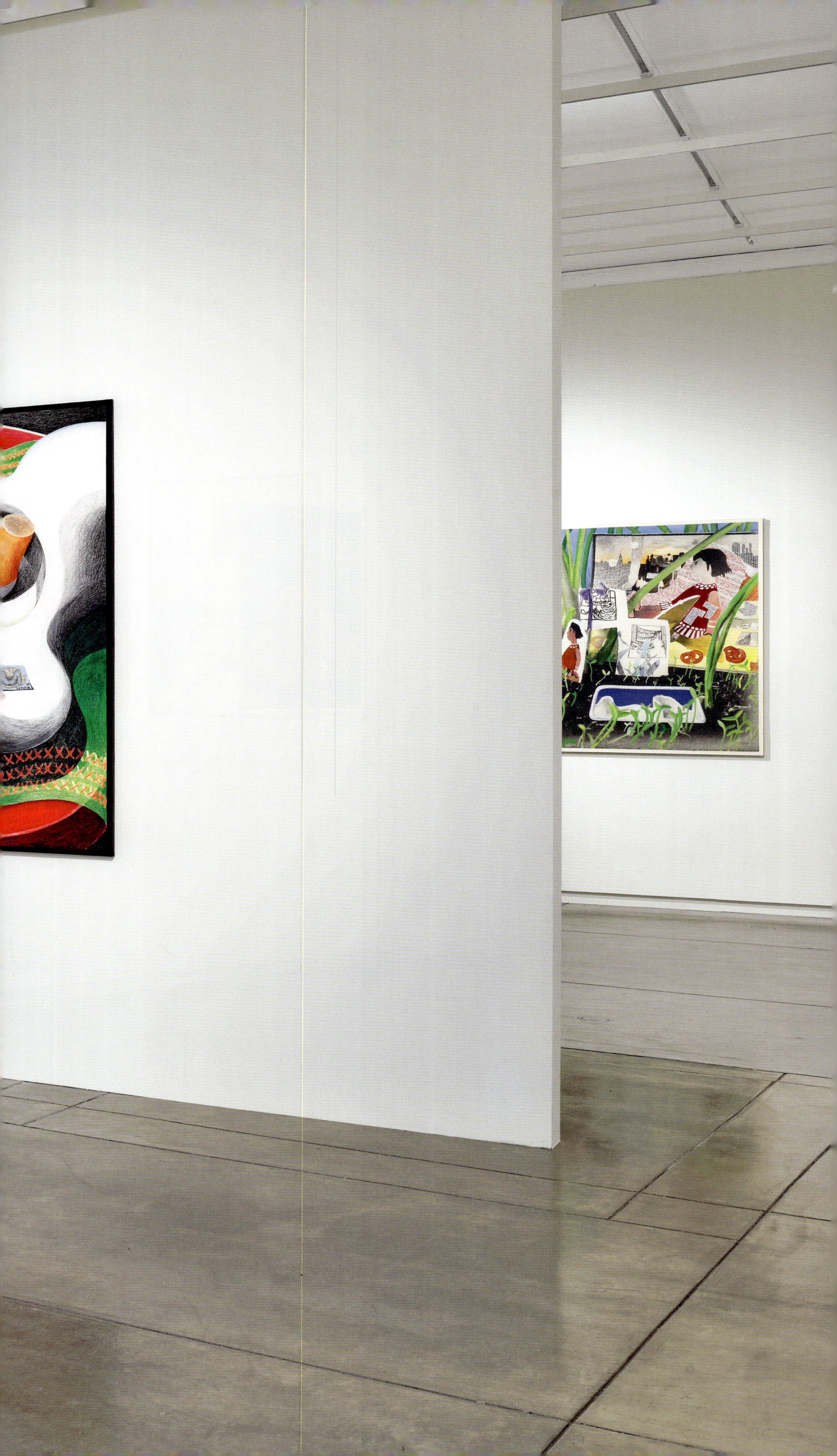

viewer could enter the picture and mentally sit at the table in front of all these things as she herself had sat there before; the viewer should become part of the situation and the dialogue with, for example, a slice of tomato.

DB So, in these drawings of her legs in front of the table, we find the tomato, but then also the cucumber. But then among the symbolic vegetables we have this abstract "thing" which appears to be an autonomous set of open legs, disconnected from the body. Or it could be intestines. A kind of independent figure reduced to this very evocative, troubling set of legs.

UV Which, of course, also had to do with Anna's life situation at that time.

DB Meaning?

UV I think it's not only about sexuality. This leg-object seems to me also a symbol for giving birth: to both an image and a child. In 1964, her son Alex was born.

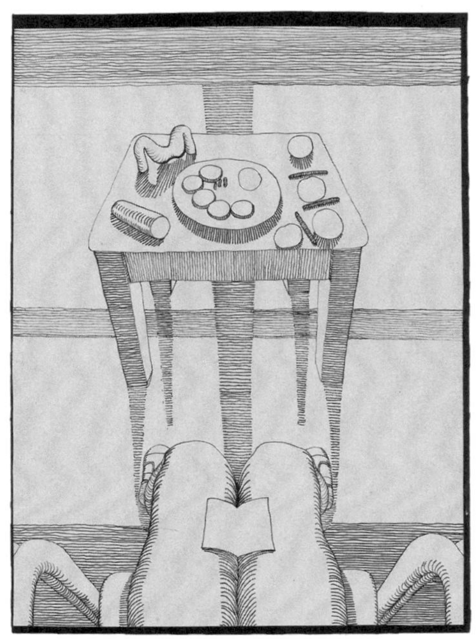

FIG. 7 *Untitled*, ca. 1968.

DB At this time in her work, there always seems to be this dual consideration of motherhood and the obligations of home, alongside a more philosophical investigation into how to be an artist, what it means to make an image and interpret the world around you.

UV I think this was really something that moved her while finding her own artistic language in the 1960s. Being a mother tied her to the house, and parallel to that she tried to overcome the oppressive expectations of society and her isolation from the art world. Another point is the female body itself: she also tried to eliminate the prison of the body. So, she let the legs become independent, she separated them from her body. In a symbolic sense she separated herself from the female belly and all related expectations concerning sex and motherhood.

DB Well, it's interesting to think about repetition as a strategy of escape or of sublimation. If you continually repeat something, you empty it of meaning. Repetition can also create an abstraction out of something, even (or especially) if it's quite visceral and specific.

UV Exactly. It's working through in a Freudian sense. And postponements. In Anna's works we can see these processes visualized.

DB This repetition, and all the fragmentation occurs within different boundaries, or frames. The idea of boundaries, of keeping the action within a container seems to repeat through the works. The container is most often the work's frame, the edges of a drawn piece of paper, or a window frame, or the frame of a mirror or tabletop, but it is also the body. The head, "opened" for us to see into, the legs, or lap, which reads almost like an open book, of elements of the home—such as curtains—which can also read as body parts such as teeth, or in this work, abstracted into a kind of energy field. And those curtains contain, or embellish, a view into another interior space, which features this strange set of open legs which reappear throughout her work. Even the most "psychedelic" motif is actually grounded in the everyday, in a curtain's subtle movement.

Then to further intensify these worlds within worlds, we see in the *Anti-Design* drawing Oppermann actually drawing little folded drawings into the picture, next to a photograph (taken at an angle so that it is set "into" the picture plane) of another drawing in this same gallery. So, in this big beautiful drawing we have both drawings of drawings and photographs of drawings. Do you have a sense of when she started to add these elements to her drawings?

UV I think that was during her work on these large condensed images. Actually, they also originate from a condensing and reviewing process. Anna started to play with the combination of contradictory dimensions. She was aware of this magic tool throughout her whole career: she could reduce things to a minimum and blow them up to the max. For example, in the cigarette picture you have this really big cigarette together with very tiny drawings. They're so tiny that one can hardly decipher them. You will find tiny little drawings and photographs throughout her whole work. Nevertheless, they are totally dense and full of meaning. Complex. Anna reduced whole ensembles with all their meanings to such small handsome images, whereas on the other hand the smallest particles were presented as huge objects.

The world loses its stable coherence with this interplay of zooming in and out. It is important to note that these changes of dimensions are never accidental and always significant. When Anna let tiny objects become monumental it is because they had a monumental meaning for her. Look again at the giant ashtray and the monumental burning cigarette. The monumentalization of these small objects to human proportions evokes the painful feeling of watching an abuse.

DB These small, concentrated photographic reproductions intensify the energy in her drawings, while maintaining a kind of diagrammatic control despite their bodily—sometimes sexualized—imagery. The table so often reoccurs as a site for display. And the window frame, or the frame actually drawn on to, or adhered with tape, around the picture's perimeters, reinforces this feeling of examination or exhibition. Experience is framed, as to be intensified, both for the action at hand as for the concentration of the viewer's attention.

UV The images all show bizarre dialogues between associatively connected objects and a subject that looks at them and arranges them. Also, the table or a pedestal to present these objects became an important visual element throughout Anna's work. The table is a device that shifts something from the ground to a higher level, that brings it into sight and makes it easier to handle.

DB A stage almost.

UV Anthropologically, the first tables were altars—and Anna always referred to the altar. She always showed her presentation tables. And moreover, she did not only show the mode of presentation but also the artist who produces, presents, and perceives. Often, we even see the drawing hand of the artist on her paper works. This way she visibly took over all roles: of the producing artist, of the curator, and of the viewer. This visible alternation of producing, presenting, and perceiving of objects, drawings, texts, photographs is maybe the crucial effect of her processual ensemble working method.

DB Can you talk about her transition from including photographs in her drawings, to reproducing drawings, and set-ups of photographs on canvas?

UV When she began with the ensembles, she soon realized that capturing the ensemble states in realistic paintings or drawings would be far too time-consuming. So, she tried out photo canvases. It accelerated the process.

DB Was this an easy technology that she had access to?

UV No, not really. It was rarely used in art in the 1960s. Anna did the developing at home. First, she worked in the kitchen, later in a small room next to the kitchen. She taped the photo canvas to the wall and exposed it from a distance with a black-and-white exposure device. Then she developed, fixed, and watered the exposed canvas in the bathtub. She used broomsticks to roll them up during the development process. So, the canvas went through the classic black-and-white development process, only that this process was more elaborate and unwieldy. For presentation, at first, she simply weighed the photo canvases down with logs and hung them in front of the wall like school maps. Later on, the canvases were stretched on stretcher bars. Nearly all of them are partially colorized. For colorization she sometimes used oil, but mostly acrylic paint. And she often added drawings and writings with felt pen or pencil.

DB I think this is an important aspect of the making process. Both for the very labor intensive method (today we tend to think of photo canvas as something cheap you send away for when you want a photo made into "art" on a canvas), and also in terms of her deep engagement with photography, even if she initially chose it as a "short cut" to avoid producing hundreds of large-scale drawings. (Even though she would continue to make major drawings and paintings for the ensembles).

UV But it was also a very toxic chemical process. She was thinking a lot about this when she got her cancer diagnosis. After that she gave up the photo development mostly and started painting again in oils. It was tragic: at that time she took on a professorship at Berlin University of Arts and they installed a huge photo lab for her where she would have been able to develop large canvasses safely. When it was finalized, she was already too seriously ill. She showed me the fully equipped lab and said, "I won't be able to use it anymore."

* * *

DB Anna Oppermann's early work here is full of beans, chives, cucumbers, tomatoes, and different kinds of plants. Nature, in the form of plants and vegetables, permeates the work.

UV She developed her own plant and vegetable "language." Each plant, fruit, or vegetable had certain allegorical meanings for her. Take for example the beans. Anna applied them as long and plump green symbols for something that is not the real problem but an *Ersatzproblem*, a substitute problem. She developed a whole ensemble on this topic since she had been accused of being too private and not political enough in her art. (The work is now at the Reina Sofia, Madrid.)

DB So, there was criticism of her work at the time as being somehow disengaged with the world?

UV Yes, indeed! In the late '60s everybody tried to be radically political, and people simply didn't see the very political dimension of her work. I would say that her work is even more political than the work of so-called political activists. Instead of presenting social utopias and current critiques from a distance, free of charge, so to speak, Anna makes the political dimension of the private realm comprehensible in all its ambivalences, precisely by not excluding herself, but showing her entanglement in the problems and conflicts. This is what is so touching.

DB People didn't see that this was a feminist critique of gender roles?

UV No, they didn't. Incredible, isn't it? But Anna herself was not really aware of this. She had doubts about whether what she was doing was really political art at all. For example, she did not consider herself a feminist. On the contrary, she refused this attribution! She called herself offensively *Künstler* instead of *Künstlerin*, i.e. she chose the German masculine form of "artist" instead of the female form. Although she refused the designation, her work is, of course, very feminist.

DB Of course! It's about emancipation, unrealistic expectations for women, the realm of the home—traditionally assigned to women—as a place of meaning and experience, and with raw, often biting and funny, critiques of normative "women's work" and sexism.

UV Yes! But she thought that with refusing the label feminist she could escape the next false attribution. She didn't want to be labeled at all. Instead, she wanted to be recognized as artist among artists and not as a feminist or female artist. Anyway, of course she realized that most people had and still do have prejudices against female artists. There was another cliché that she feared even more: to be looked at as a female artist and housewife, a type that connects naïveté and dilettantism. So, she presented this attribution as a trap in her early pictures, as well as in *Being a Housewife*. She hoped to escape it by reflecting it.

DB So back to beans and such. These were things she observed, were in her life?

UV Yes. For example, the ensemble *Being an Artist* was initiated by windblown linden blossom petals that landed on her table when she was sitting on a balcony. She started thinking about artists' attempts at representing nature and sketched the petals while

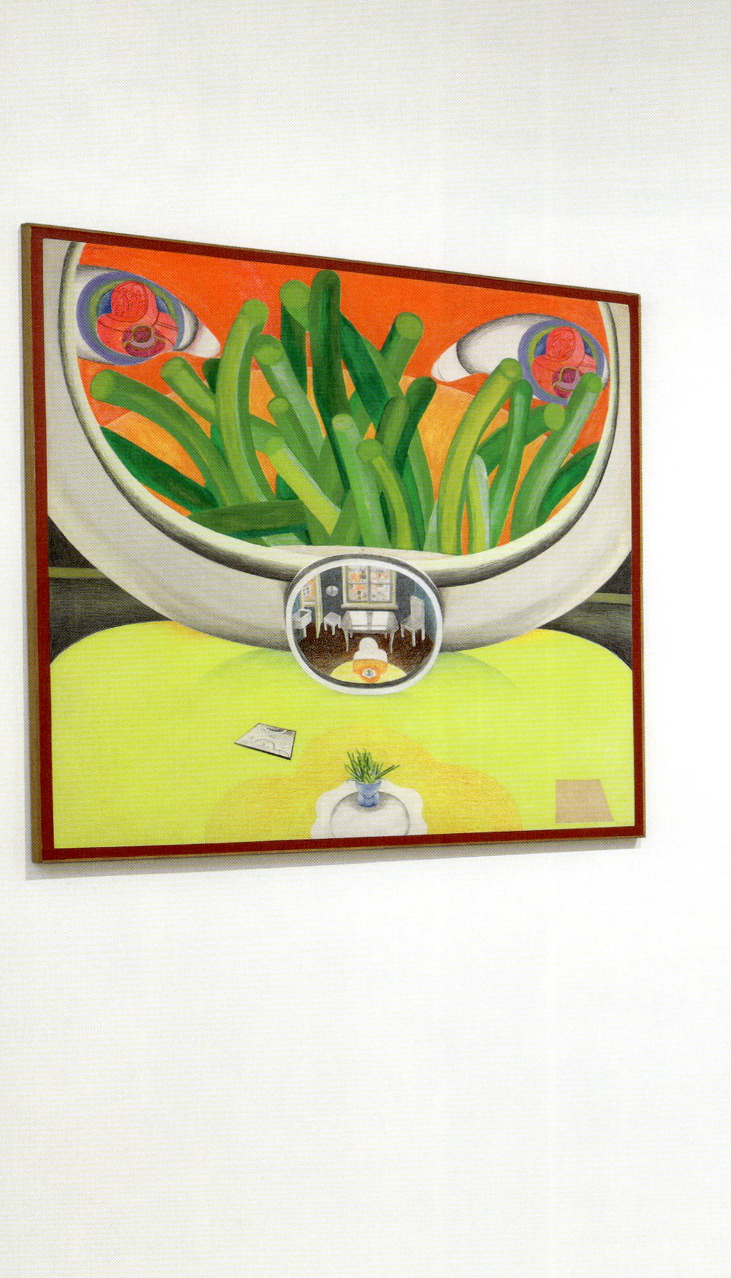

Being a Housewife, 1968/1973
Being a Housewife (1968/73), one of Anna Oppermann's first installations—or "ensembles"—connects her drawing practice to the room-filling, image based installations for which she would become best known
Here, Oppermann began to explore the oppressions and tensions she felt as an artist who was also expected to be a housewife. Mirrors and windows—vital motifs suggesting the possibility of transport to another dimension, and articulating boundaries between inside and outside—appear in her ensembles as well as her drawings. Often beginning with a small makeup mirror, she constructed her ensembles through an observation of optical reflections, using the mirror to duplicate, shift, and expand the perception of interior space to be reflected from multiple, often overlapping viewpoints
Banal objects came into her life, took on expanded, subversive meanings, and found their place in ensembles, with plants carrying special symbolic value, the prickly cactus a stand-in for the "housewife" figure. Combining objects, drawings, photographs of drawings, and photo-canvases of her ensembles into each installation, Oppermann borrowed equally from the display methods of museums, informal memorials, home interiors, and retail environments. The profusion and overlap of images and portals, and the visual estrangement of familiar things, connect Oppermann's (and the viewer's) interior world to a home environment of simmering, chaotic complexity hiding in plain sight.

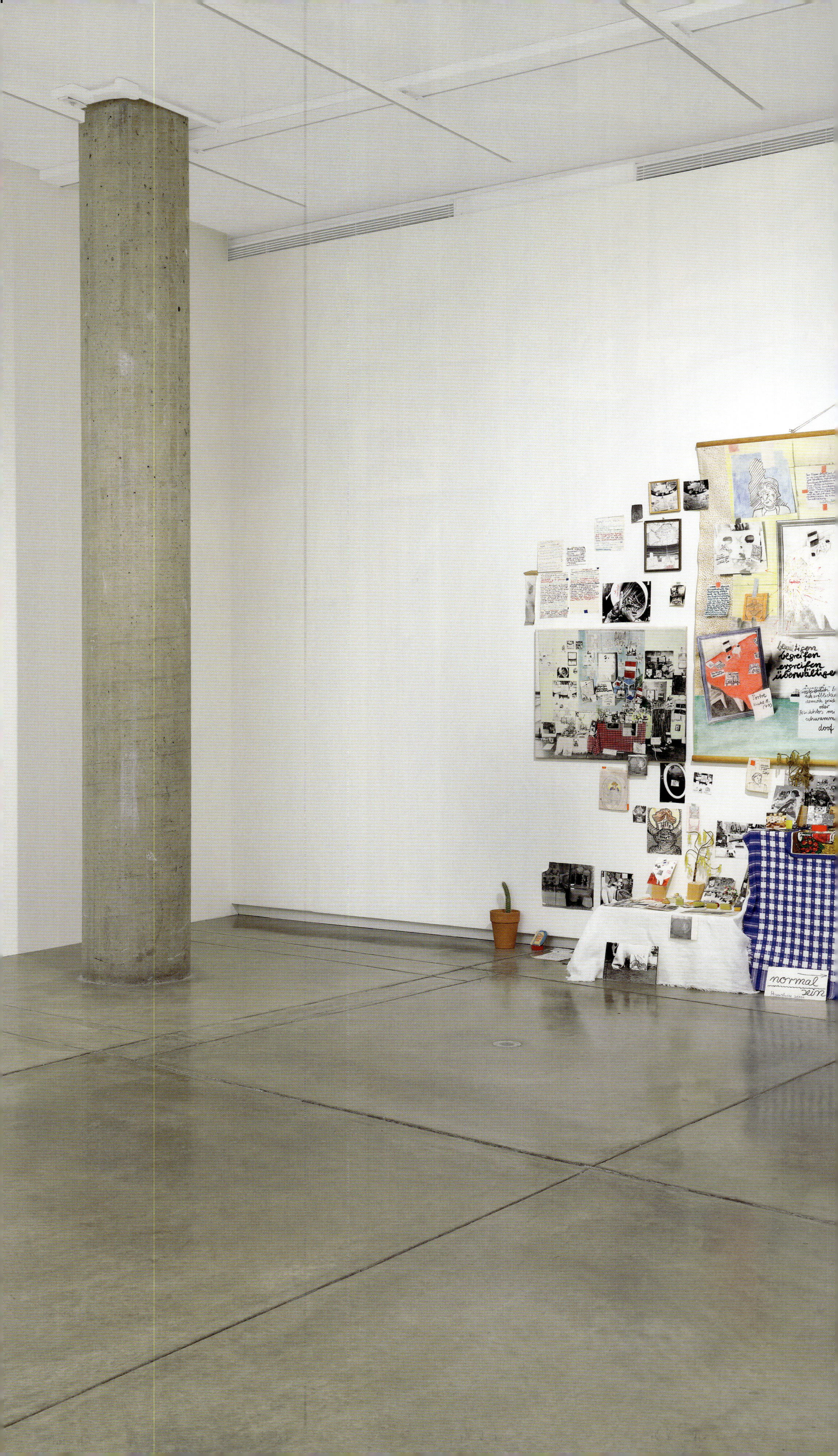
begreifen
ergreifen
doof
normal
sein

reflecting on this. Sometimes she also took on the symbolic meanings of a certain plant, like, roses for women and love. For herself, she chose the tulip as a symbolic flower. Tulips are special. They are more everyday flowers—"kitchen flowers," very different from roses. And they still grow after being cut. Their leaves become very thin and tender when they dry. I guess this fragility touched her. There is a small ensemble about tulips, but you can find them everywhere in her work. In *Portrait of Mr. S.*, a work about love and eroticism, there are red tulip petals. In later works, like *Paradoxical Intentions*, there are white ones. And, of course, chives and cress she found in her kitchen. She created quasi landscapes out of them. Look at this little Indian girl sitting in the cress on the canvas over there. Like in the fairy tale of Thumbelina.

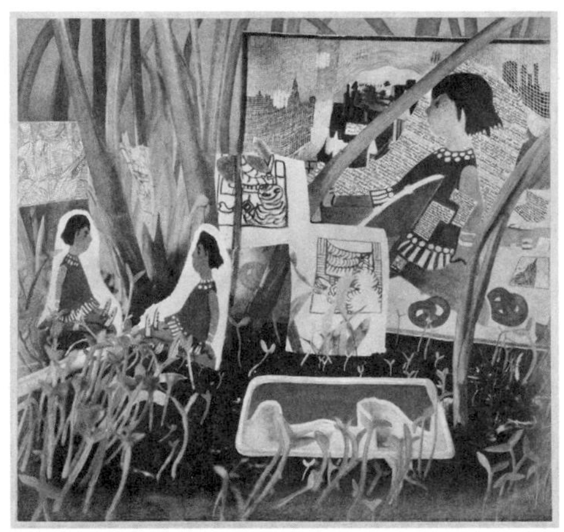

FIG. 8 *Mirror corner*, 1968/1970.

DB Let's look at the ensemble *Being a Housewife*, one of the reasons we chose this work for the show is that it's such an early ensemble, made while she was making the drawings we are also showing. But it also begins to bring the motifs, perspectives, and methods of the drawings out into space through the combination of photographs, objects, drawings, and other materials. Maybe you could say something about this transition from the drawings to the ensembles, and how they existed together initially.

UV The ensemble appears to be a collection point for a whole series of motifs that we see in the neighboring gallery. There is, for example, a picture of a crying housewife in the other gallery and some others who are trapped in check patterns. Finally, the ensemble is Anna's way of breaking out of the prison. She let the situation explode, literally. On the central photo canvas, she has painted an explosion of kitchen furniture.

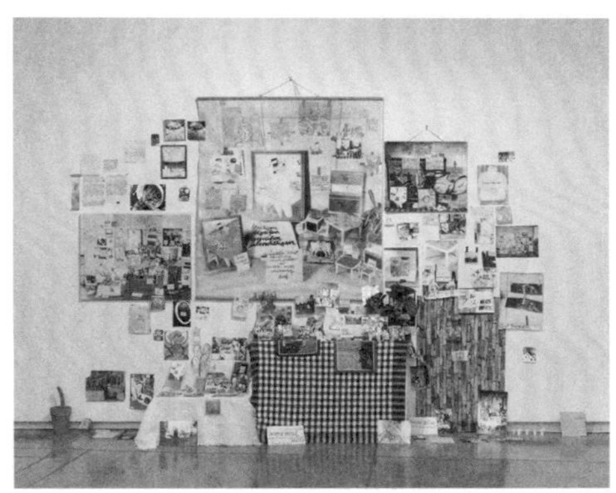

FIG. 9 *Being a Housewife*, 1968/1973.

DB One can sense an aesthetic of frustration, or of a kind of additive energy, that the artist is layering and adding until she arrives at something resembling the state of simultaneously occurring ideas, experiences, and perspectives she means to convey. These tabletops, which in the drawings used to be ordered, legible stages for activity, are now teeming with an organically expanding force which actively delays "reading" and clearly distinguishes the subjects of each photograph or small drawing. The previously distinct identity of surface or display structure and depicted objects start to intermingle and confuse.

UV The ensemble makes the picture itself explode. It looks as if the explosion took place in the central picture and then the particles were spread out over the wall and into the room. But it's less installation, than a relief.

DB Exactly. It's not "immersive." It's not around you. It's still a thing with edges. And it's still somehow an image.

UV Yes, since it's based on pictures. The ensemble shifts between the second and third dimension. It's very three-dimensional when the viewer is close. But when you step back, the contours blur. You can no longer decide exactly what's on a picture and what's in the room. In this ensemble she has also attached drawings and photos to the canvas frame, resulting in some overlapping. In later works she rarely did that.

DB There's a wonderful, delicate observational drawing here, depicting her knees from above, up against the edge of a table. One can read this as a careful, descriptive predecessor to the more stylized, mysterious drawings in the exhibition. As Oppermann discussed, she started from a kind of clear-eyed observation of herself—her body—and its immediate surroundings. And from there, things got interesting. Here's the source image of Lydia, the housewife in the other gallery.

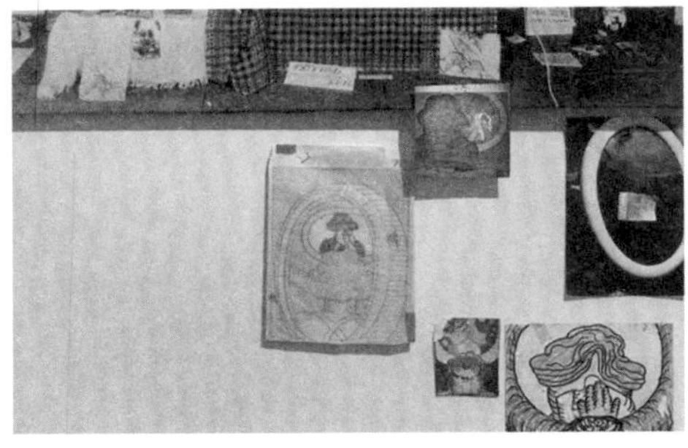

FIG. 10 *Being a Housewife* (detail), 1968/1973.

UV She's forty-two. Lydia is forty-seven, and here is also Christa B. Anna wrote *Portre* on this sketch, which is an incorrect spelling of the word portrait and hints once more at the supposed naïveté of women.

DB So, in terms of her process, in order to arrange all of these photographs in the ensemble, she would set it up in her studio, photograph it many times, and then include those photographs of the ensemble in the "final" presentation?

UV You see this here: the background of this central canvas is her kitchen wall. In front of it she first set up the doll furniture, which we see repeated throughout. And then she taped the drawings and photographs to the walls. Well, today we wouldn't do that because the photographs and drawings would disintegrate. Instead, we use these very tiny nails. But for Anna, the tape was an easy way to attach the drawings and photographs so she could move and remove them quickly. So, we have all these shifted images, and of course they represent different temporal layers, starting with the initial set up of the doll furniture.

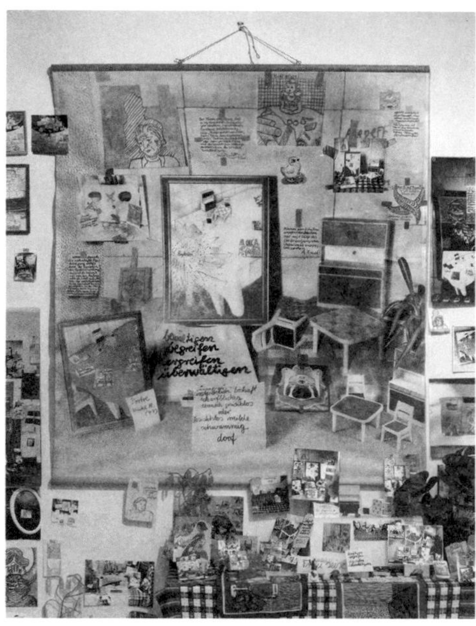

FIG. 11 *Being a Housewife* (detail), 1968/1973.

DB So, it starts there, but she would have perhaps changed it the second time she installed it?

UV Well, it always changed. There are also elements of it that she definitely produced after the last public exhibition at the Kunsthaus Hamburg, in 1972. This means that the question of the housewife was still of interest to her later on and it seems to me as if she had planned to exhibit the work once more. She made this new photo canvas which shows the ensemble in the exhibition in 1972 to replace a canvas that is no longer held by the estate. But then the work seems to become less important to her. Other conflicts and problems moved and engaged her more. I say problems or conflicts since I don't like the term "theme." She never looked for themes. She only dealt with questions that she herself was concerned with and in which she was involved. But in 1984, when she planned her first and only retrospective during her lifetime, she once more worked out something new for *Being a Housewife*.

DB For the exhibition catalog?

UV Yes. This was about twelve years later. She made these cutout figures which are sitting behind a window in a room made of paper. We look from the outside in through the window frames. I have decided to put these photographs into the ensemble—even though Anna never exhibited them. But in my mind, they would have been missing since they are a part of the work—albeit a late part.

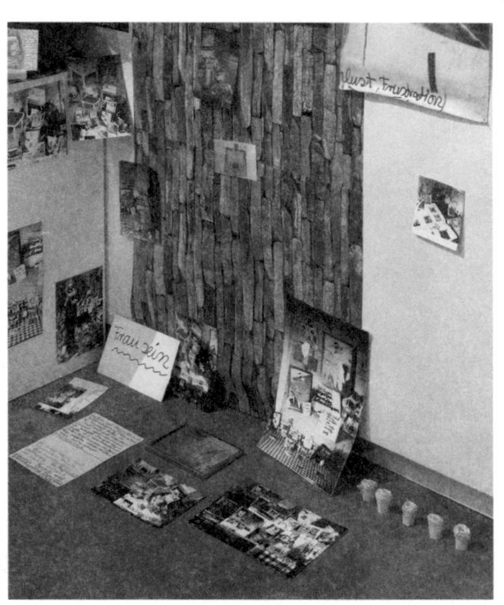

FIG. 12 *Being a Housewife* (detail), 1968/1973.

DB So, when you were working with her, you would help her set up the ensembles or what was your task?

UV I was never her assistant. I wrote my PhD about Anna's work and so I had a scientific interest. But Anna couldn't stand that really.

DB She didn't want you to be a critic, or like an art historian, while observing the studio work?

UV In a way, she felt supervised and restricted by my attempt to explore her work. And she just could not stand somebody watching her working. She said, well you can come when I am installing an ensemble, but then you have to help. So, I got involved in the installation. She asked me not only to write a short explanation but also a text in watercolors on cardboard. I was nervous since I knew that these texts would become part of the work. And they are still part of the work, which now belongs to the Hamburg Kunsthalle. So, within an ensemble there is not only her handwriting, she always included other people's handwriting, too.

DB I see, so she would tell you what to write?

UV Yes, she told me to write a certain text. And when I asked how I should do it she answered: "Write it as you want to write it."

DB Ah, in your hand.

UV That didn't make it easier. Just ask Herbert Hossmann, her life companion. He had to write a lot of texts for her. But in the early works, it's mostly her own handwriting. She discovered later how interesting different handwritings are. And to have other people writing also saved some time during the installation process.

DB So, you were doing handwriting and then physically setting up the works with her too?

UV It was one of the last installations that I accompanied her on. And she had other people helping to set it up. She was already ill at that time. But shortly before her death she asked me to install an ensemble. She was invited to take part in an exhibition in Munich and she no longer had the strength to realize it. I fended that off reflexively, but she insisted. She had installed that ensemble in her house in Celle, Germany, where I was visiting her. I asked her what she expected me to do. She simply said: "Look at the piece and how I did it. Do it similarly." That was the only instruction she ever gave. And I remember this every time when reinstalling an ensemble. Reinstallations are never copies but interpretations. Similar, but always different; altered, but in a way that she might have done it. In the end we didn't realize the exhibition in Munich since she died right at that time. But since 1993 I've successively learned by doing and redoing to interpret and reinstall her works according to her working method. Of course, I learned by making a lot of mistakes. I realized that the freer I got in the copying, the better the final result was. But to come to this point you first have to study all of an ensemble's former states as well as all its particles. You have to find out what is the aesthetic rhythm of this very work and which particles are important. Even though Anna repeated her working method the aesthetic impact of each ensemble is different from the other. By the way, everybody who is willing to get intensely into Anna's work should be able to do interpreting reinstallations.

DB Did she work with an assistant earlier in her life?

UV Actually, the only real assistant whom she ever had was Herbert Hossmann. He was absolutely great since he supported her on all levels of work even though he had a fulltime job as a lawyer in public administration. He helped Anna with the organization of exhibitions as well as with packing art, stretching canvasses, or writing texts. He accompanied her to all the exhibition installations and was with her during her illness. And after her death it was because of Herbert that today her work is still visible and alive. Since 1993, when we started to develop appropriate ways to conserve and exhibit the ensembles we are in a constant and constructive exchange.

DB Is this her?

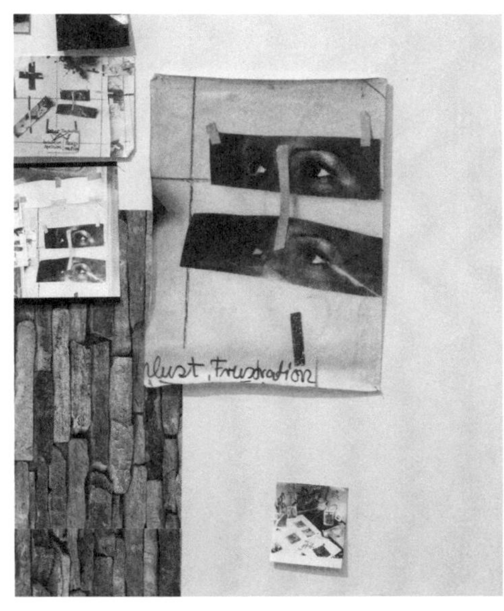

FIG. 13 *Being a Housewife* (detail), 1968/1973.

UV Yes, those are her eyes. This is such a strong visual element: a pair of eyes, cut out and taped to the kitchen wall. It looks as if the person is behind the wall looking out through a slit. It took me a moment to realize that it's only tape stripes.

DB Let's have a look at this little frame. What does that say?

UV That's the viewfinder I mentioned earlier. Anna added, *Es ist nicht deutbar*, which means that it cannot be interpreted. Next to it you have this sad, dry flower. And here we have the viewfinder again. Actually, this is the frame of a makeup mirror into which she placed a picture. And over there we have another interesting clue: We see the artist mirrored in a cup of coffee.

DB Ah yes, eyes and nose formed by lines in the coffee.

UV Above the drawing she has written *Frühstückskaffee*, breakfast coffee. The husband is already gone for work. You see his empty dishes, but, look, the direction of the knife …

DB … Is pointing at the housewife, and she's just having her coffee and seeing herself.

UV The lonely housewife sees her face mirrored in her coffee.

DB A whole relationship and the whole world contained in this little cup of coffee.

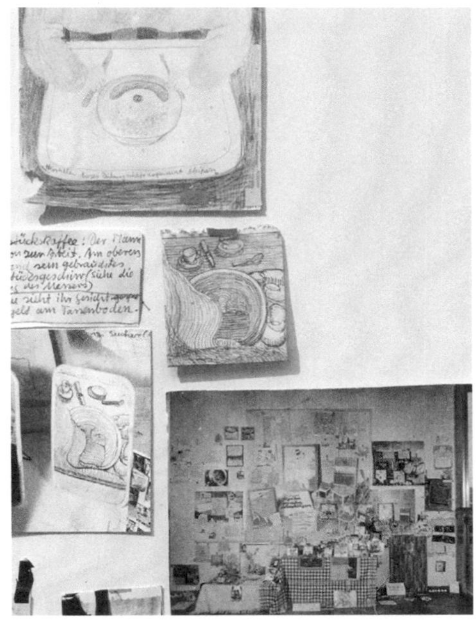

FIG. 14 *Being a Housewife* (detail), 1968/1973.

UV One has to get very close to the work to see that. She also added quoted fragments of texts from Germaine Greer, Sigmund Freud, and Anna Freud. These are quotations which she found—or which found her, like the other objects. They deal with female stupidity and inferiority. Freud, for example, declares the "indubitable intellectual inferiority of so many women" as prerequisite for sexually oppressing them.

Stupid women make things easier for men. Tough stuff. In the end it is all tough stuff. Because she also did not suffer with the female victims. Women seem often *gesichtslos*, as Anna noted here. Faceless.

Like Christel, twenty-two. You can find her over there at the age of forty-seven. And that's really interesting, because at the age of twenty-two she's surrounded by food and crockery. At forty-seven, she's surrounded by artworks and drawings.

DB So, age forty-seven seems to be better …

UV Well, definitely!

Being an Artist

Meta Marina Beeck

In the Beginning

Anna Oppermann—born Regina Heine in Eutin, Germany, in 1940—moved to Hamburg at twenty-one to study at the Hochschule für bildende Künste (University of Fine Arts Hamburg, today known as HFBK-Hamburg), with the goal of earning a degree in art education. In Paul Wunderlich's graphic arts class she met her future husband, Wunderlich's teaching assistant, Wolfgang Oppermann. Oppermann, who was three years older than Anna, was already a well-known artist in Hamburg; his objects, graphics, and painting were strongly influenced by Pop art and the New Objectivity.[1]

Early on in her studies she produced a series of collages on Masonite, the expressivity and composition of which recall Dada and Art Informel. In *Untitled* (1963), a child's doll sitting in the lower left half of the picture immediately catches the eye; oddly twisted, missing its right leg, its eyes turned upward, the doll seems to add collage elements to the lead and colored pencil drawing. Two tightrope walkers, another naked baby doll, cross motifs, a clock, and the figure of a sleeping woman in the upper half of the picture provide clues to the themes.

The processing of autobiographical events is quite evident in the work. Regina Heine and Wolfgang Oppermann were married on August 14, 1963, and a year later, on October 21, 1964, their son Alexander was born.[2] In another collage, Oppermann addressed the fears and misgivings alluded to in *Untitled* (1963) more specifically.

1 See Klaus Gallwitz, ed., *14 mal 14 – Junge deutsche Künstler*, exh. cat., Staatliche Kunsthalle Baden-Baden (Baden-Baden, 1968), n.p.

2 In about 1967 Regina Oppermann began signing some of her works as "Anna Oppermann." Regina, which stems from the Latin word for "queen," felt too pretentious to the artist.

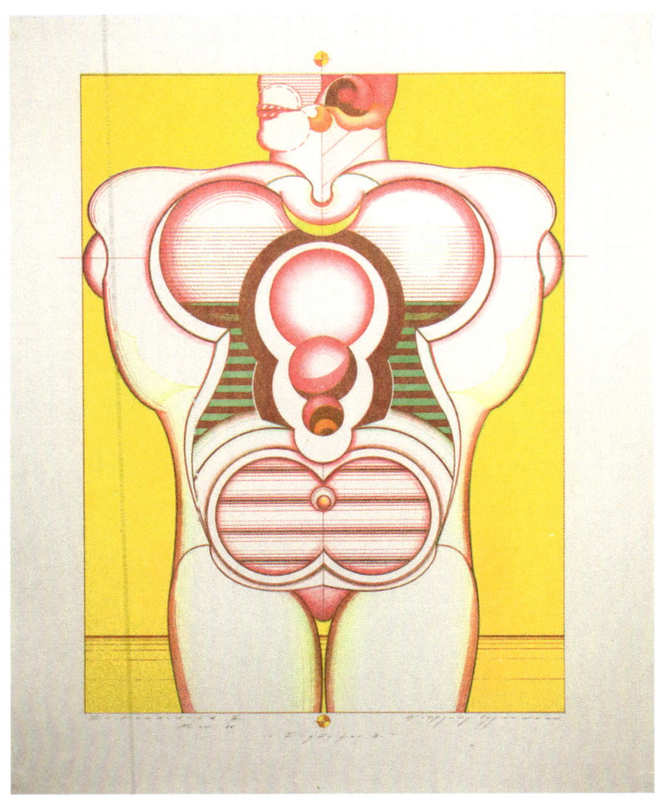

FIG. 1 Wolfgang Oppermann, *Figur der Kreise* (Figure of circles), 1966. Color lithograph.

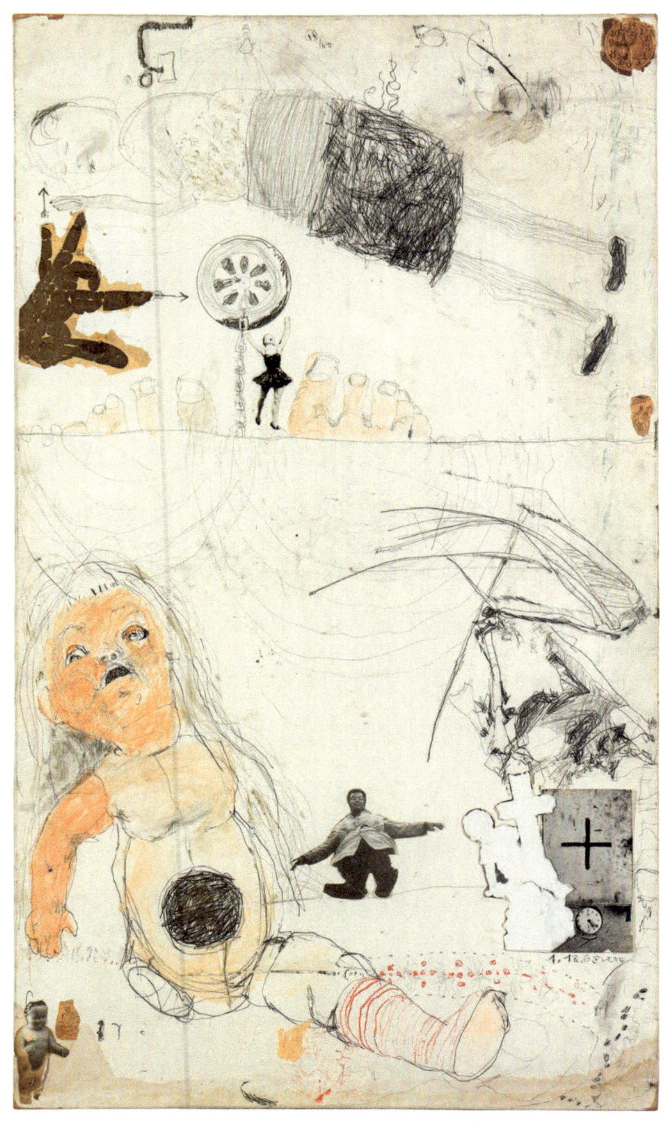

FIG. 2 Anna Oppermann, *Untitled*, 1963. Collage, pencil, colored pencil, and gouache on Masonite.

This work, dated December 15, 1963, features the handwritten comment, "life goes on without me," introducing some of the central themes of her oeuvre, which examined questions concerning the compatibility of work and family, individuals, fears and social expectations, dreams and reality, as well as issues of failure and loss. A somewhat later drawing in colored pencil features a central reclining figure. Only a pair of trouser legs, spread wide in the air, can be seen. Lying on a pedestal and surrounded by various oval frames, the person seems both exposed and lost. Written in green colored pencil in the middle of the picture, the words *Isolierung 69 A. O.* (Isolation 69 A. O.) serve as a signature and a description of the scene, while also noting the mental state portrayed.

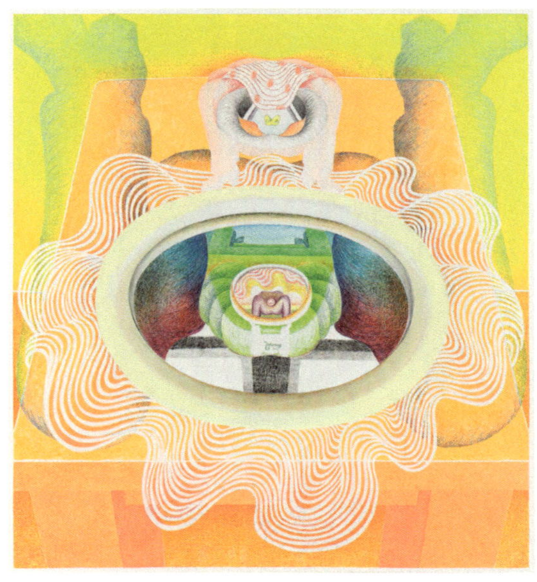

FIG. 3 Anna Oppermann, *Untitled*, 1969.

The experiences of being excluded, of being defined by others, and denied recognition can be said to characterize a great deal of art made by women around this time. Marionette or doll-like figures appear in Hannah Höch's photo-montages, collages, and paintings; as disempowered, lifeless, and deformed extras without any free will, they seem to have been deprived of any opportunity to develop. As one of the few female Dada artists (a movement we think of as progressive) Höch fought for recognition as a woman and an artist. It was necessary to reject the corset of the middle-class family that expected women to be loyal, caring mothers and efficient housewives. With her 1919 collage *Bürgerliches Brautpaar (Streit)* (Bourgeois newlyweds [Quarrel]) Höch caricatured this restricted view, showing a constrained female figure with a child's head, in front of a tapestry of kitchen appliances resembling instruments of torture. The discrepancy between society's idealized, traditional image and the individual's pursuit of a self-determined life are themes that have often engaged women artists in the twentieth century.

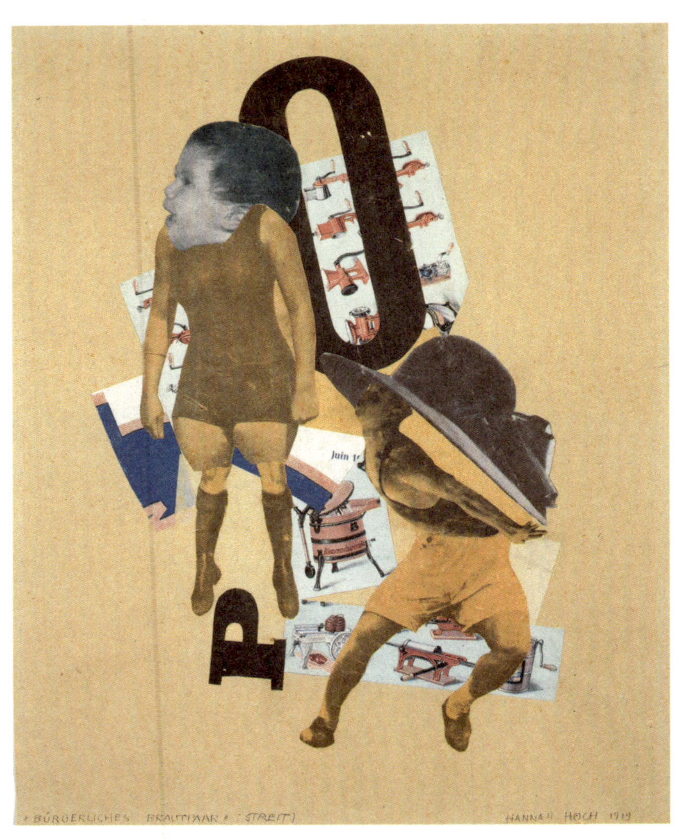

FIG. 4 Hannah Höch, *Bürgerliches Brautpaar (Streit)* (Bourgeois newlyweds [Quarrel]), 1919. Collage.

In contrast to the more troubling psychological themes sometimes explored by Oppermann in the early 1960s, the influences of pop culture, consumerism, and the media are very strong in a series of drawings and paintings made between 1965 and 1968. The brash, bright colors; the scenarios that recall states of intoxication and fantastical dream worlds; and the motifs taken from youth and music cultures fuse to create surreal, overflowing landscapes of materials, as well as interconnecting worlds of images that absorb the viewer. In a colored pencil drawing, Oppermann portrays the musician Frank Zappa, a rare instance where the artist depicted a real figure from popular culture; a symbol of the pop, underground, and counterculture of the 1960s and '70s.

After 1965 Oppermann's look inside the body evolves into a kind of introspective research. Conducted through the artist's process of self-observation, it alternates between anatomical studies

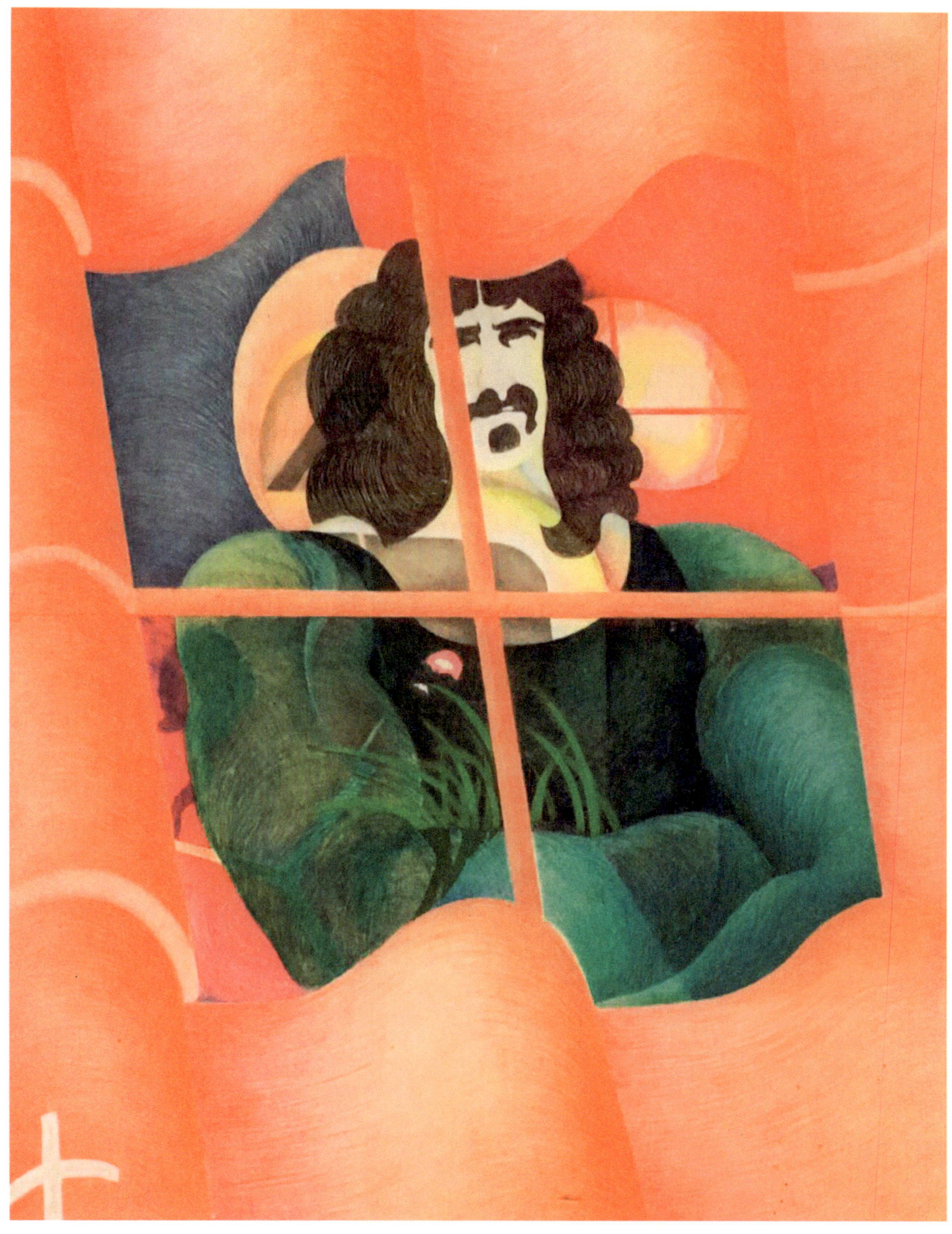

FIG. 5 Anna Oppermann, *Untitled (Frank Zappa)*, 1968/1969. Colored pencil, felt pen, pencil on cardboard.

and fantasy worlds the penetrate the psyche. In her work *Untitled*, ca. 1965–68, one can see into the body of a nude, female figure. Instead of a head, the body opens up into a view of a bare tree in front of a truncated window frame. The image, however, can also be interpreted as a synapse, with the structure and shape of the "pathways" that determine the human brain's physiological activity. The woman's arms are positioned slightly forward, and on another level of the picture two oversized hands are attached to them. These hands seem to be grasping at nothing. However, at the same time they lead toward a vanishing point at the center of the picture, where there is a green cross in between the green trouser legs of a figure bending forward. A scaffolding of colorful bars blocks the view of a landscape, indicated by branches and twigs, in front of a blue background. Pictorial space opens up into an inwardly directed depiction of a landscape. The easel painting functions like a "portable window," by creating an illusion of depth and emphasizing the picture frame with its "window-like edges." "The frame of the easel picture is as much a psychological container for the artist as the room in which the viewer stands in for him or her," explains the conceptual artist Brian O'Doherty, equating its shape with an invitation to the eye to step inside the painting. The illusory pictorial space is revealed as "foreground, middleground, and distance" for viewers, pulling them into the picture window, with the suction effect varying according to the intensity of the tonality, the style, and the depth.[3]

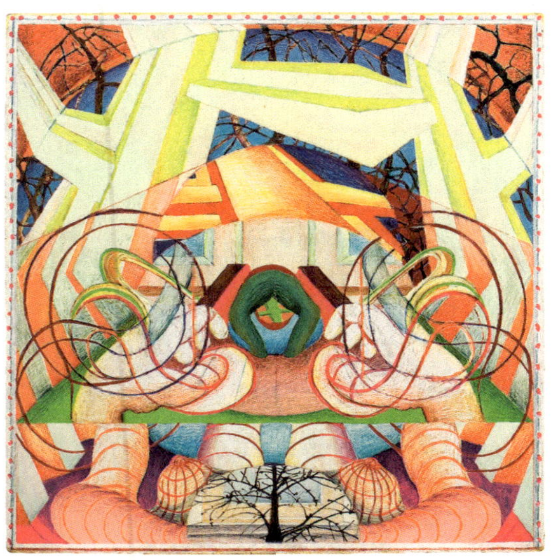

FIG. 6 Anna Oppermann, *Untitled*, around 1965/1968.

Anna Oppermann uses the mirror as an instrument that opens up a distant perspective and, like a window, directs the gaze toward a landscape outside of the picture itself. The mirror became a leitmotif for the artist:

3 See Brian O'Doherty, *Inside the White Cube: The Ideology of the Gallery Space* (Berkeley: University of California Press, 1999), p. 18.

> For me, the mirror, the exclusion of reality, was a crucial event. I take a mirror, and there is reality around the mirror, and the reflection of reality in the mirror, which stands in contrast to the reality surrounding the mirror. This transforms the frozen "reality" in the mirror, transported from one place to another, into an image. The reality reflected in the mirror is alienated by the way it is framed. There is something about it that is poetically irrational and stimulates the imagination.[4]

As a motif, hands jutting out into space appear in many of Oppermann's works. The hand mirror opens up the space into a surreal visual world and in this sense, it functions as a passage of interlocking pictorial planes.

The strongly self-reflective metaphor of the mirror is an overarching theme in twentieth-century art. Identity is inseparable from perception and due to the artist's loss of identity, its construction is left up to the viewer, who is, for example, forced into the role of the artist. Eliminating the artist by making her identical to the body of the spectator is an approach to empathetic perspective that Oppermann deploys when she presents the cut-off knees in a seated position, reaching into the picture, as an invitation to the viewer to assumer her perspective.

A preliminary catalogue raisonné assembled by the artist herself reads, "mostly paintings and drawings until 1968; since then, ensembles of objects, photos, drawings, paintings, and photo-canvases." Oppermann described her three-dimensional works of art as ensembles, which now stretched out beyond the two-dimensional easel painting into three-dimensional space. The material she gathered and arranged according to a fixed method comprised drawings, photographs, sketches, newspaper clippings, personal commentary, copied quotes, and other found objects. She described her process of creating these idiosyncratic installations as follows:

> I constructed still lifes in order to create a picture (as painters have always done), did sketches, was rarely finished with the image (which was considered a failing), took photos of individual phases and at some point

[4] Quoted in Ute Vorkoeper, *Anna Oppermann: Ensembles 1968–1992*, exh. cat., Württembergischer Kunstverein Stuttgart (Ostfildern-Ruit: Hatje Cantz, 2007), p. 126.

> arranged everything in order to be able to better compare still life and translation.[5]

What had merely been alluded to in the early work through the choice of perspective and the use of collage, Oppermann now transferred to real space. In a certain sense, she refused to employ the compositional intervention of setting boundaries, by negating the constraints of the picture frame, which dictates a focus, in favor of an open-ended collection of material in space. Expanding the traditional pictorial space has been attempted by various artists, from the Cubists to Marcel Duchamp to Robert Rauschenberg. In the 1960s, Rauschenberg—who had been making assemblages since 1953—started making his "combine paintings." His piece *Bed* (1955) is made up of a blanket with a pillow attached to the canvas and painted into the composition. Slightly later, the Swiss artist Daniel Spoerri began making his object-art paintings (or "snare pictures"), which also included everyday items in their composition. None of this represented a final split from the panel painting, however. The dissolution of the boundaries between art and life, for which Dada and Surrealism paved the way, developed significantly in the 1950s. With new art forms such as performance art, the happening, and the environment, Allan Kaprow was one of the first artists to transform the exhibition space into an accessible, experiential arena, turning the spectator into an active participant. One of the artist's environments, in the Smolin Gallery in New York, is made up of the leftovers of a happening. Participants in the happening *Words* (1961) were asked to write down their thoughts on strips of paper and attach them to the wall. Read like notes, the words turn the internal external and make the viewer aware of the current of thoughts among the happening's participants at the time of the event.

"Emancipation Versus Manipulation!"

The first extensive presentation of Oppermann's ensembles took place in 1972 at the Galerie Kleber, in Berlin. At the invitation of Manfred and Andrea Kleber, Oppermann exhibited works that expand beyond the classic two-dimensional format into the space.

5 Quoted by Anna Oppermann in *Identität – Versuche bildhafter Selbstdefinition*, Thomas Kempas, ed., exh. cat., Haus am Waldsee (Berlin, 1974), n.p.

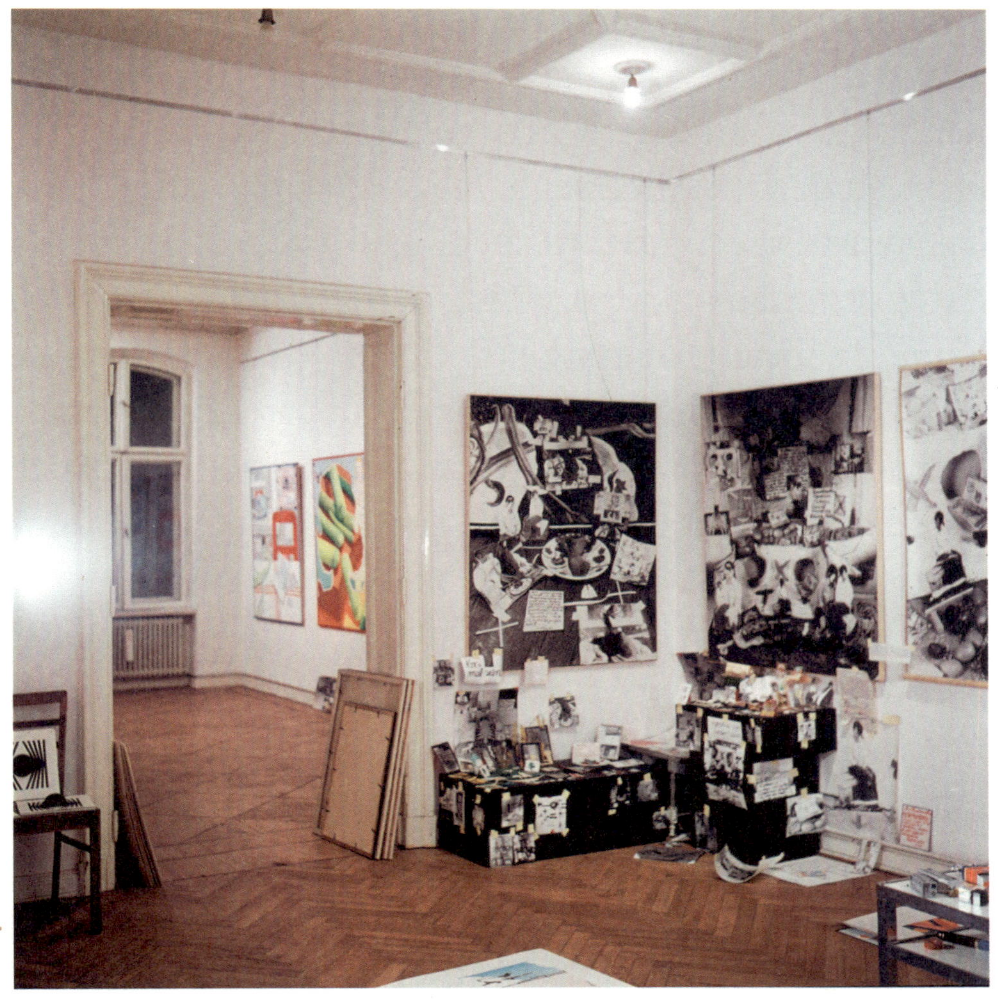

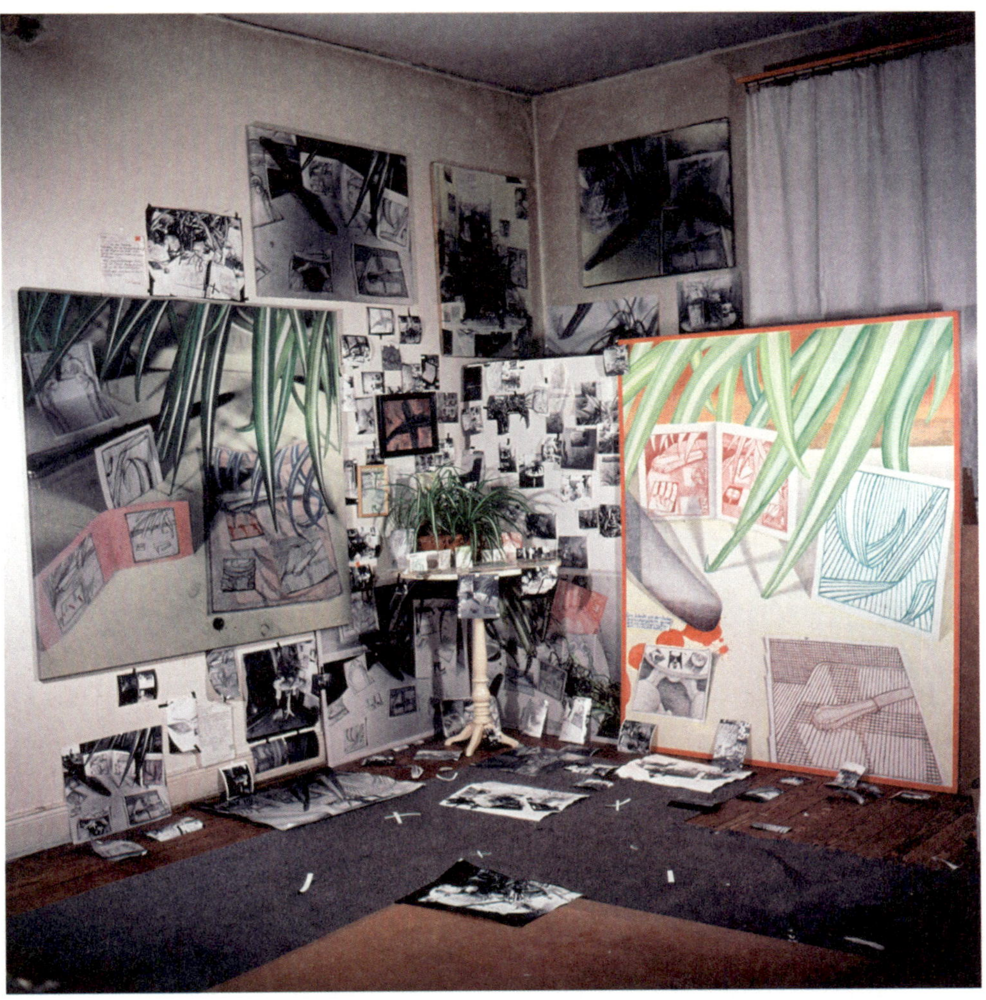

FIGS. 7, 8 First solo show at the Galerie Kleber, Berlin-Charlottenburg, 1972.

The invitation to the show identified five thematic groups: "1. Normal sein (Herr Stangl mit 30 Jahren), 2. Anders sein (irgendwie ist sie so anders), 3. Frau sein (mischi pischi), 4. Künstler sein (Zeichnen nach der Natur) 5. Ich sein (muß man)."[6] An additional comment on the card specified: "on 1, 2, 3, and 4 ways of life, states of consciousness, which in the way they are presented to me are infinitely repugnant to me," which summarized Oppermann's motivation. Questions about career and family, as well as individual fears of not measuring up to society's expectations are depicted in her early work. The stereotypical, bourgeois ideas of society in the 1960s were the bogeyman to many female artists, and Oppermann dealt with the traditional image of the woman in a multipart complex of artworks. For example, *Frau sein (mischi pischi)* (Being a Woman [mischi pischi]) fanned out in her later creations of various solo ensembles. *Hausfrau sein* (Being a Housewife), *Gurken und Tomaten (Frau sein)* (Cucumbers and Tomatoes [Being a Woman]), *Frauen wie Ängel* (Women like Angels), and *Antidesign* are some of these early ensembles. The materials assembled in them range from toys, kitchen utensils, cosmetics, decorative objects, and packaging to newspaper quotes, women's magazines, and theoretical writings that explore the position of the woman in society and the manipulative mechanisms that encourage the stereotype of housewife and mother. Via the pieces selected and the comments compiled, it quickly becomes clear how early childhood education—alongside culture and consumerism—participates in constructing the image and function of women. In the figure of the Avon lady, the profitable system behind the beauty, cleaning product, and kitchen appliance industries is shown to be occupational therapy for the bored housewife and an essential capitalist market.

In Germany the cosmetics company advertised their house visits in the 1960s with the slogan "AVON brings beauty directly to the home!" In various works, Oppermann describes the visit from an Avon representative to Lina P., a housewife, commenting on the "never-ending, cutesy chatter" and how "the birdbrain thinks and thinks and broods in a tidy home." The models featured in Avon advertisements conformed to the conventional idea of beauty at the

6 1. Being normal (Mr. Stangl at 30), 2. Being different (she's somehow so different), 3. Being a woman (mischi pischi), 4. Being an artist (drawing according to nature), 5. Being myself (must be). Mischi Pischi is a semi-nonsensical phrase roughly translated as "pussy pee."

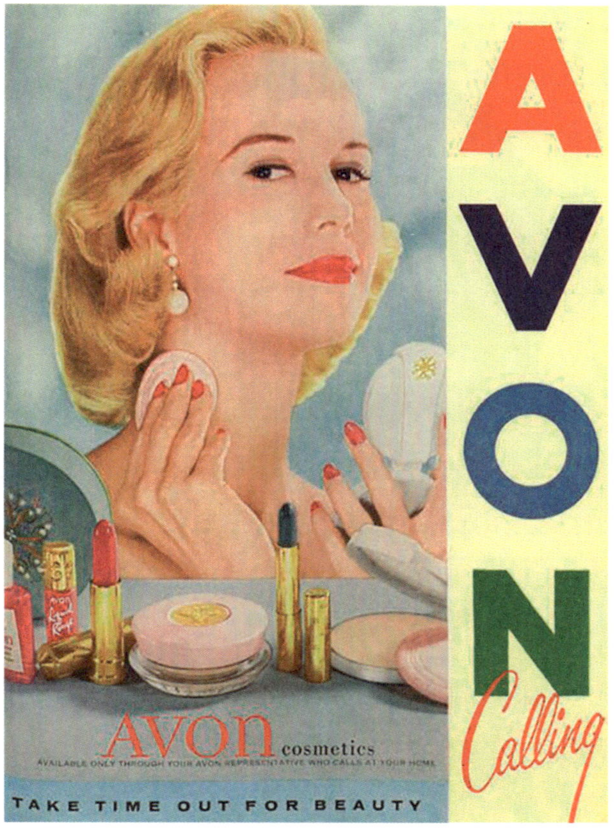

FIG. 9 Avon advertisement from the 1960s.

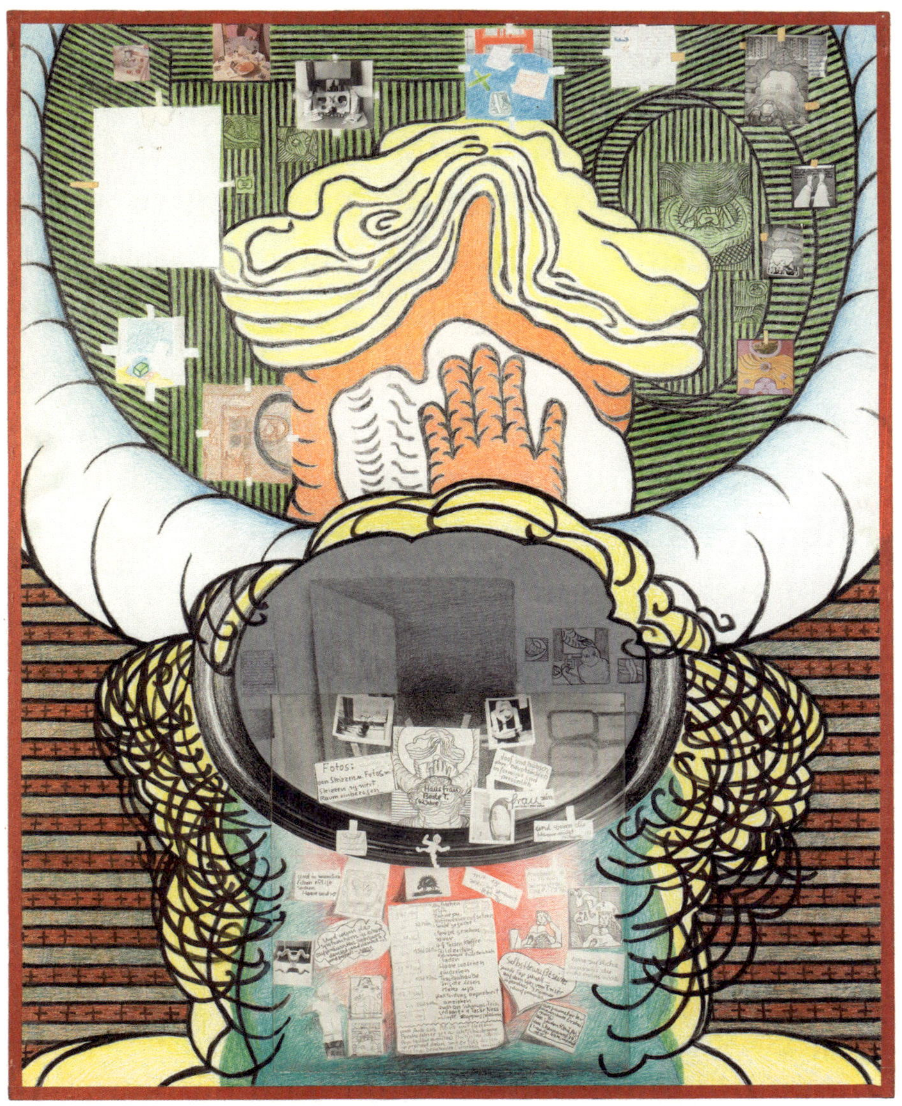

FIG. 10 Anna Oppermann, *Ohne Titel* (Untitled), around 1968. Mixed media on Masonite.

time: blond, backcombed, shoulder-length hair, a made-up face, and an innocent, yet seductive, smile.

A teak angel, a decorative yet superfluous object gathering dust on the dresser, and other angelic figures that appear in *Frauen wie Ängel* (Women like Angels; 1968–1973)—which originate in a middlebrow, illusory world characterized by compulsions and lead to an idealized image of "woman"—reveal the standards one is forced to deal with.[7] These images, produced and distributed through advertising and consumerism, make use of Pop art. Confronted with an increasing flood of visual materials and a growing palette of products that populate an exciting and fulfilled life, the woman who is constantly observing and correcting herself is herself transformed "into an object, very particularly into an object to look at—into a 'spectacle.'"[8] Discussing *Frauen wie Ängel*, which preceded the ensemble *Frau sein (mischi pischi)*, Oppermann said,

> Naturally, the title itself is meant ironically. It implies, as one can say in concrete terms, my exploration of the female image, the female role, the external appearance of women, the aspiration I never fulfilled. Of course, I did not include myself personally. But it firmed up the conflict and a confrontation with this other type of woman (her norms, coiffures, her behavior), which I did not admire, but which is accepted and demanded by society, which felt superior to me, which hounded me, and then quietly wore me out.[9]

In a handwritten CV found among Oppermann's papers, she mentions a seminar taught by the British Pop artist Allen Jones, which she audited during the winter semester of 1968–69. Jones was exhibiting at documenta 4 that year and had been invited to teach at the art school in Hamburg. Three years before, Oppermann had attended a lecture given in Hamburg by the American Richard Lindner, who

7 The word *Ängel* is wordplay that combines two German words—*Ärger* (anger) and *Engel* (angel). *Frauen wie Ängel* expresses the tension between an idealized image of a gentle woman and the circumstances under which women can cause (or experience) anger and trouble if they don't correspond to that stereotype.

8 Quoted in John Berger, *Sehen: Das Bild der Welt in der Bilderwelt* (Hamburg, 1988), p. 44. Originally published as *Ways of Seeing* (London: Penguin, 1972).

9 Quoted in Anna Oppermann and Herbert Hossmann, eds., *Anna Oppermann: Ensembles 1968–1984*, exh. cat., Kunstverein Hamburg (Hamburg and Brussels, 1984), p. 49.

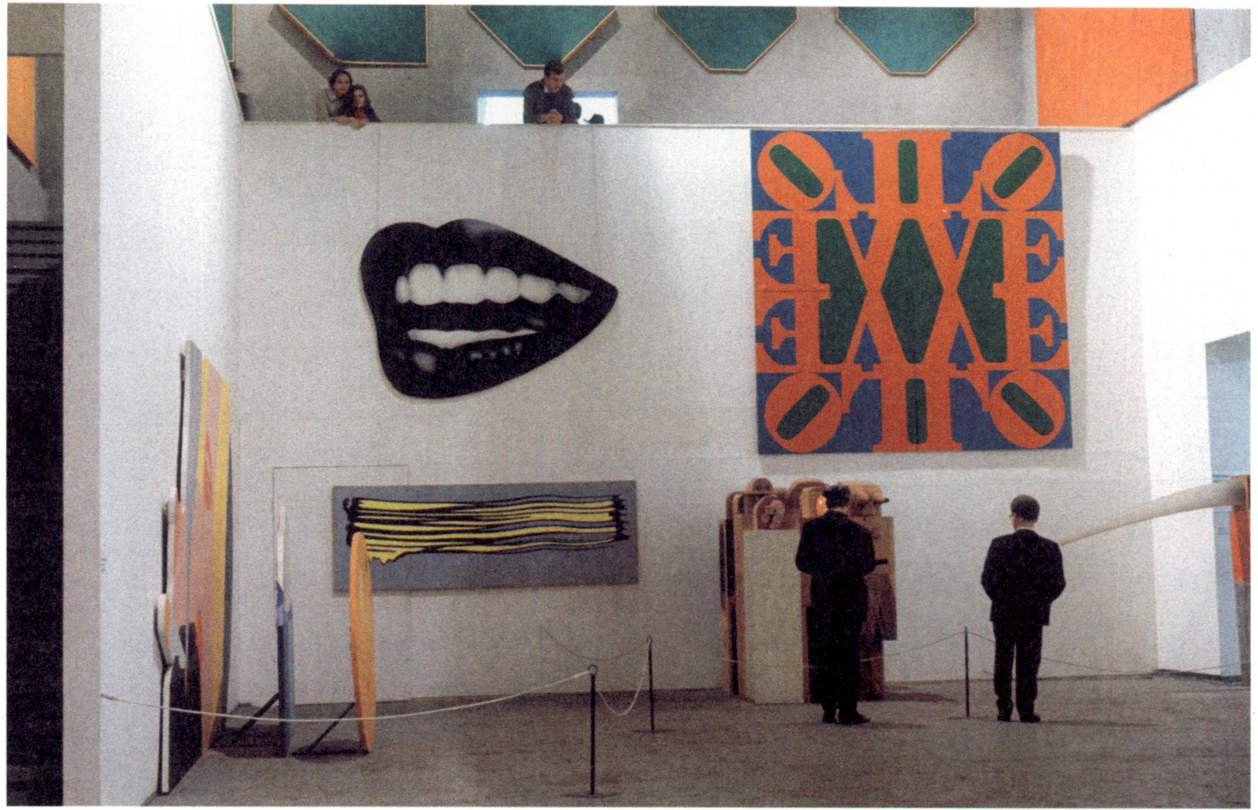

FIG. 11 Installation at the Fridericianum, documenta 4, 1968, with (from left) Tom Wesselmann, *Great American Nude No. 98*, 1968; and *Mouth No. 15*, 1968; Roy Lichtenstein, *Yellow Brushstroke II*, 1965; Robert Indiana, *The Great Love*, 1966, and others.

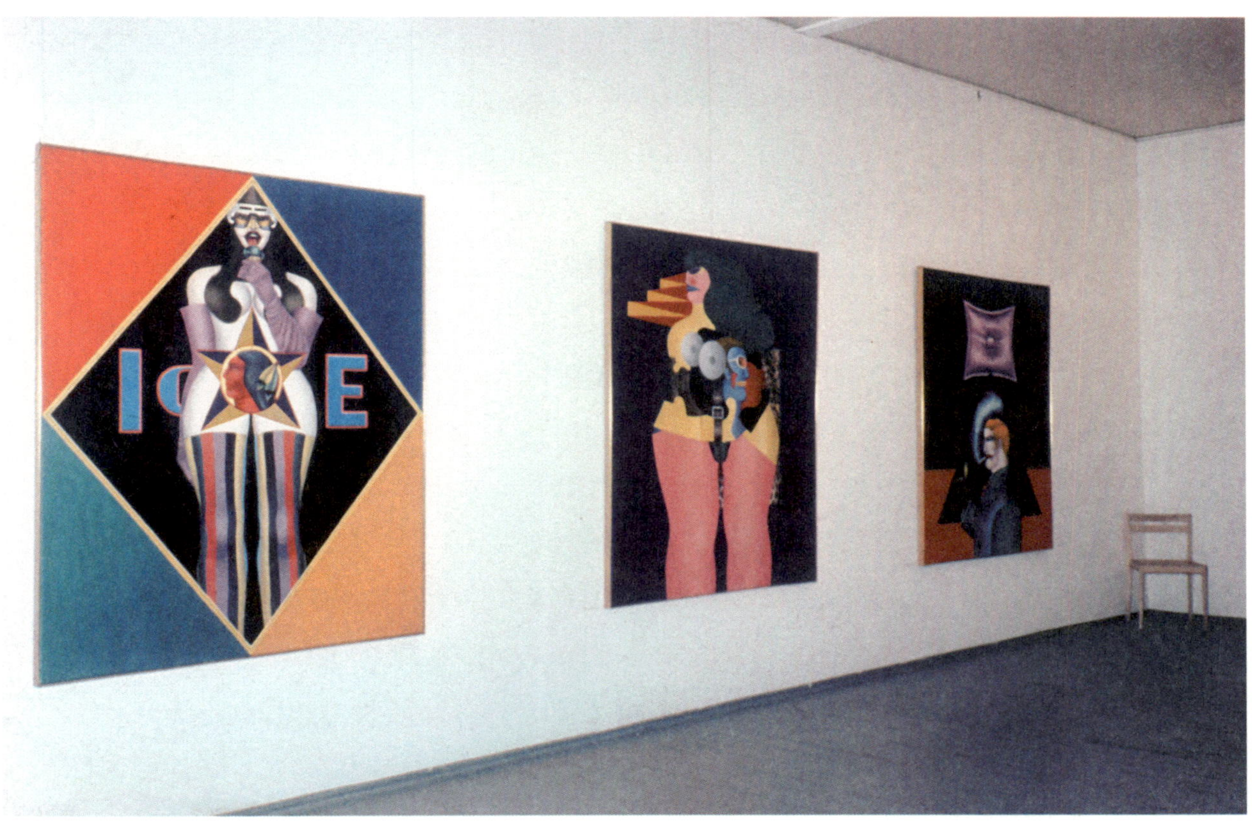

FIG. 12 Installation: documenta 4 in Kassel, with Richard Lindner, *Ice*, 1966; *Leopard Lily*, 1966/67; and *Pillow*, 1966.

was also a guest professor at the Hochschule für bildende Künste. Pop art was one of the clearly recognizable focal points of documenta 4 in 1968 (the last documenta curated by its founder, Arnold Bode). Allen Jones held one of the most significant and visible positions in the large-scale exhibition. Aside from Allen Jones's *Perfect Match* (1966/67), a ten-part series of Andy Warhol's *Marilyn Monroe* (1967) was on display, as well as Roy Lichtenstein's *Big Modern Painting* (1967), Tom Wesselmann's *Great American Nude No. 98* (1968), and Robert Indiana's *The Great Love* (1966). Richard Lindner also exhibited a few of his works in Kassel. In particular, Jones' sexually provocative nudes of women in high-heeled shoes and erotic poses drew attention.

In 1969, Jones produced a series of erotic sculptures. The lightly clad fiberglass sculptures depict seductively posed women, inviting viewers to sit, lie, or place something on top of them. These "dolls," dressed in sexy lingerie, black gloves, and knee-high leather boots, have been turned entirely into objects. Reduced to decorative furniture and for the pleasure of men, the sculptures initiated a heated debate, led by feminist critics, after their first public presentation in 1970. The film critic Laura Mulvey aired her anger in a 1973 essay, which was published under the title, "Fears, Fantasies and the Male Unconscious; or, You Don't Know What's Happening, Do You, Mr. Jones?" and described the work as "life-size effigies of women, slave-like and sexually provocative, doubl[ing] as hat-stands, tables and chairs."[10] The theme of the ensemble *Antidesign* (1970–72) was a form that had already appeared in early drawings, but which now evolved into functional objects (furniture, vase, ashtray). It is the image of what seems to be a woman reclining with her legs spread wide. This image can be interpreted in accordance with Mulvey's critique, especially when Oppermann comments in felt pen on the ensemble *Gurken und Tomaten (Frau sein)* that the degradation of women to the status of a (seating) object is equal to the "the status of woman in today's society. Psycho + socio-symbolism." The reduction of woman to a sex object, and the Pop artists' unlimited enthusiasm for consumerism and the advertising industry that reinforced the stereotyped, clichéd roles has been attacked by numerous female

10 From Laura Mulvey, "Fears, Fantasies and the Male Unconscious; or, You Don't Know What's Happening, Do You, Mr. Jones?" in Mulvey, *Visual and Other Pleasures* (Basingstoke, UK and New York: Palgrave, 1989). Originally published in *Spare Rib* (1973), p. 6.

artists since the 1970s in the battle for the authority to determine how women are depicted in art and media. The process of breaking down clichés by exposing their alienating and oppressive function consists of showing how deeply they are anchored in society, for one, and investigating the consequences to the individual so indoctrinated, for another.

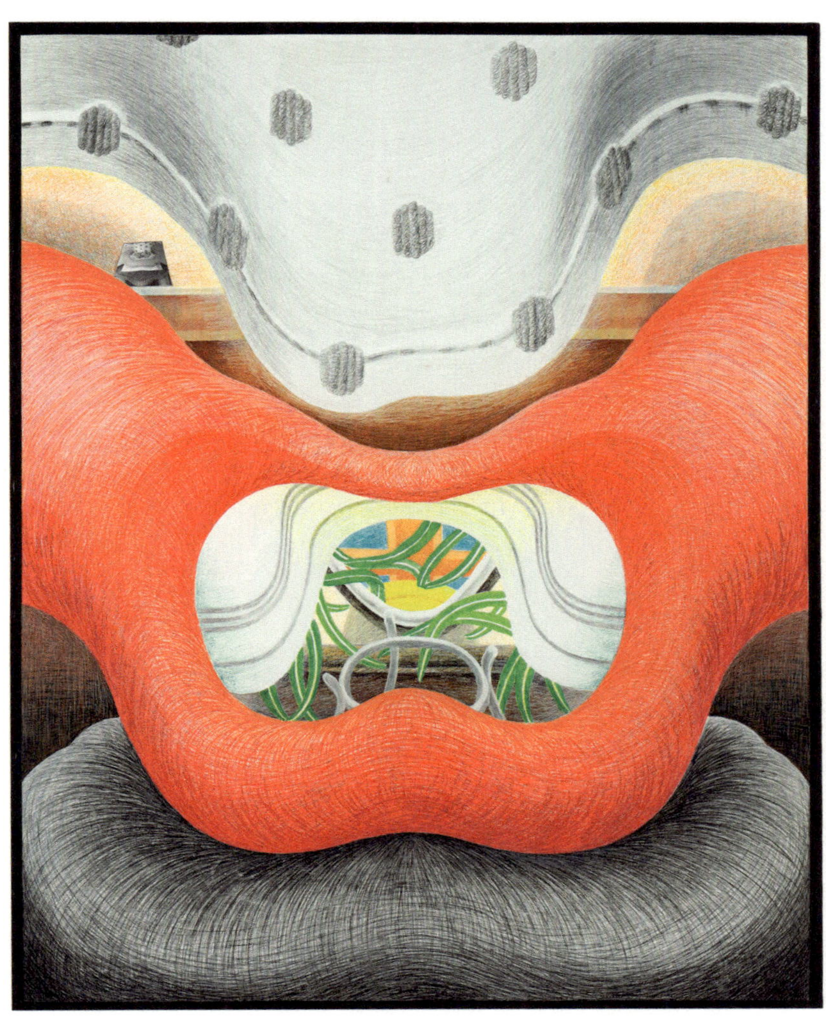

FIG. 13 Anna Oppermann, *Red figure with curtain*, 1968.

With the women's movement of the 1960s as a backdrop, and the increasing efforts of female artists to reject the patriarchal structures in educational and exhibiting institutions, Oppermann's works seem to be part of a personal battle for visibility, denouncing the retrograde state of affairs that affects society. Both the housewife and the career woman are confronted with preconceived expectations. In Oppermann's brief portrayals of the fictional life stories of housewives Lina P. and Beate T., or of the career woman

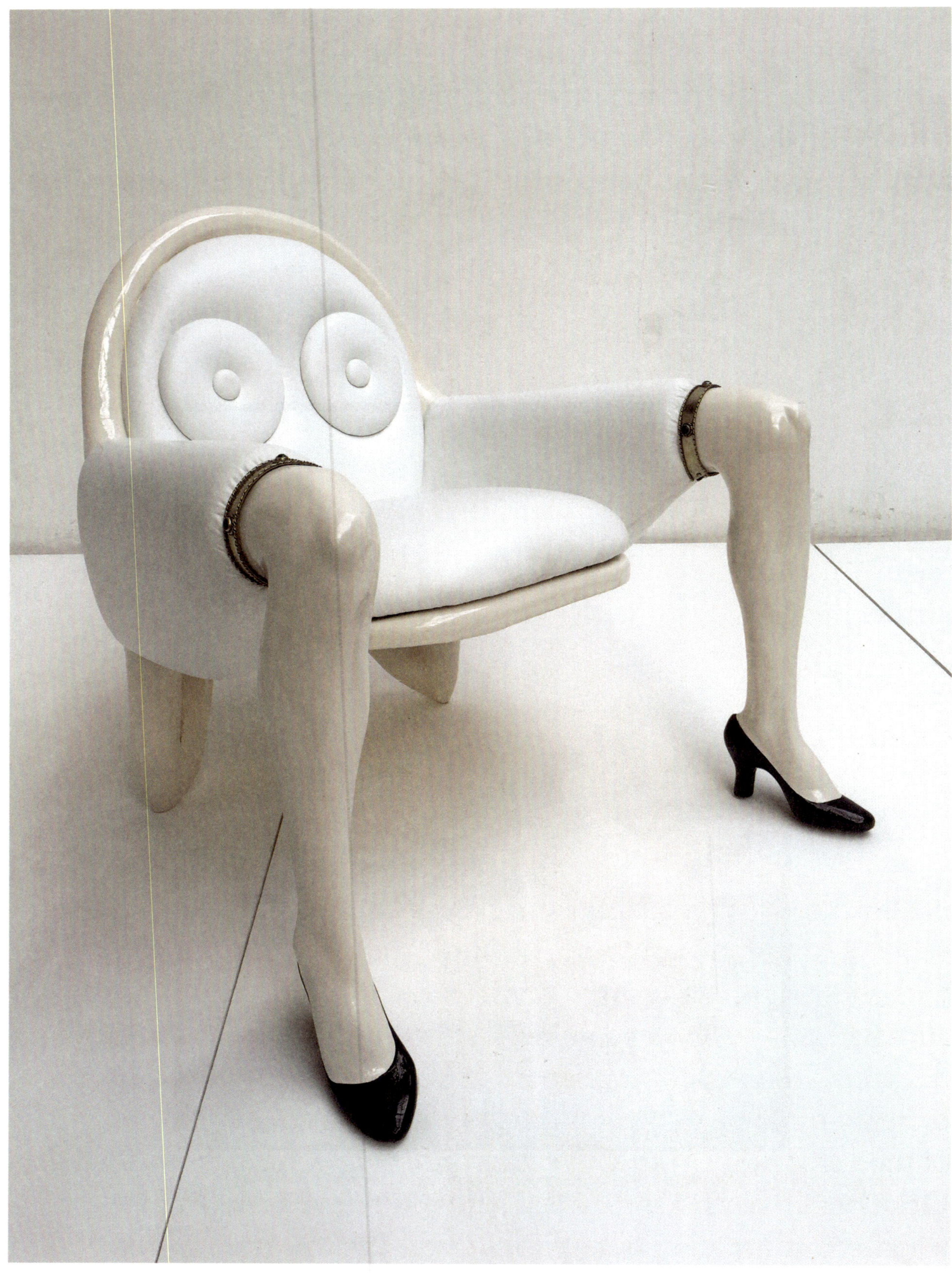

FIG. 14 Anthony Redmile, *Body Chair*, around 1975. Upholstery on a Fiberglass frame.

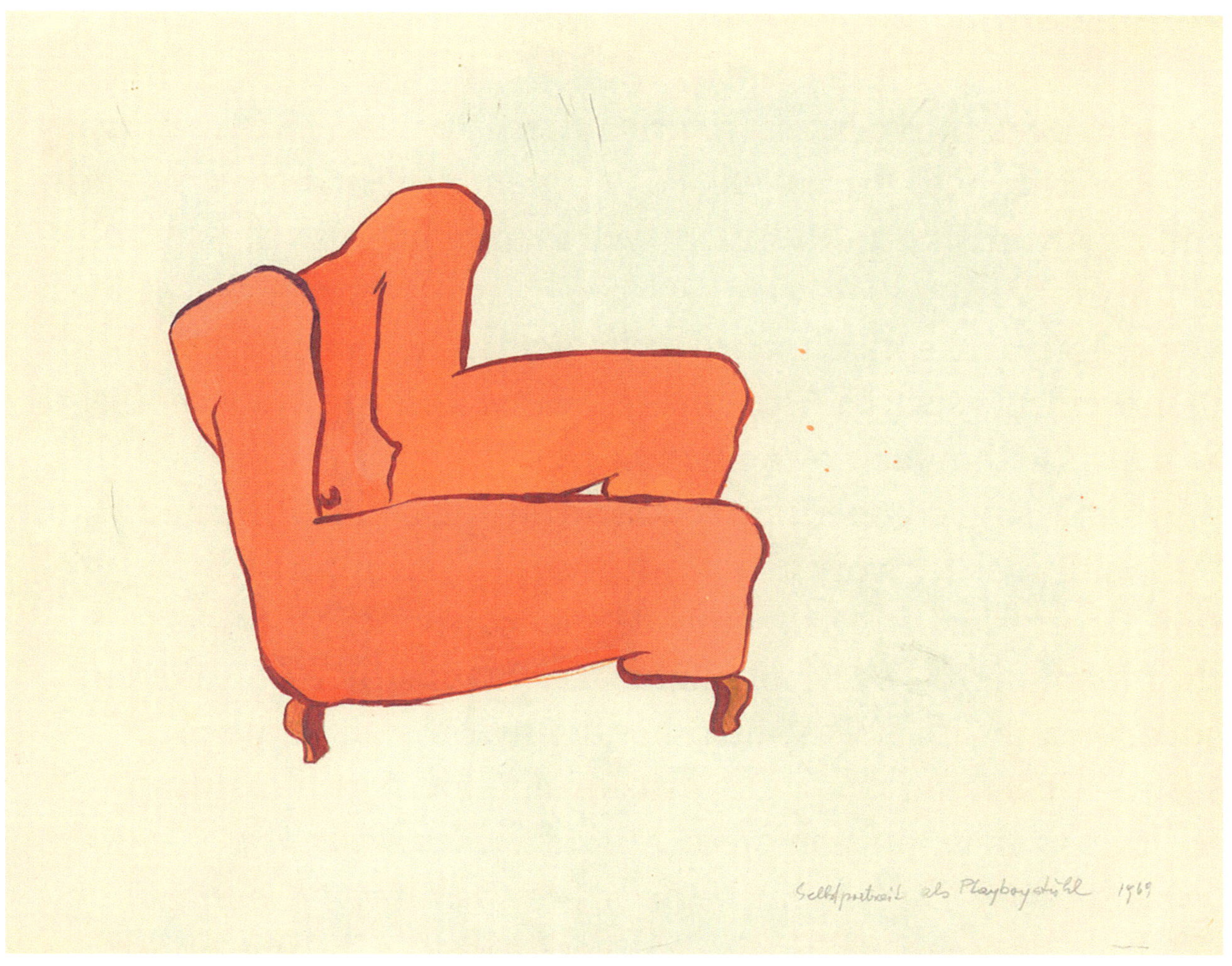

FIG. 15 Maria Lassnig, *Selbstportrait als Playboystuhl* (Self-portrait as Playboy chair), 1969. Gouache.

Nanine, the narration cites the rigid structures of faceless lives that serve as status quo conformity. The realization that, in contending with these rigid model lives, one's own way of life is judged, and automatically leads to a conflict that is Oppermann's overriding dilemma. Figures in her pictorial worlds become painfully aware of being trapped, of the limitations placed on the development of the personality, and of the corresponding definition by others. Oppermann feels that the bleak, monotonous life of the housewife, who finds affirmation through shopping and the gazes of strange men, is just as much a prison as the golden framework in which the ambitious career woman moves:

> "Nanine is the editor-in-chief of an elegant ladies' magazine — a career woman, charming and clever. Now she looks thoughtfully out of the gold frame of the image that ornaments the cover of her third little book." [11]

11 Quoted from *Avonberaterin zu Besuch bei Lina P.* (Avon saleswoman visiting Lina P.), 1968.

Disappointed by the lack of reforms after 1968, the 1970s saw many artists retreat into private life. Pop art's enthusiasm for consumerism and its advertising aesthetics, as well as minimalism's purism and affinity for technology, were replaced by artists producing personal work that was skeptical toward technology. They found each other in movements such as Arte Povera, *Spurensicherung*,[12] conceptual art, as well as within their own mythologies.

Increasing competition in the art market, which affected the conditions for work and production, led many artists into isolation, depression, and economic deprivation. In 1979, under the direction of Uwe M. Schneede, the Hamburger Kunstverein collaborated with artists and other figures on Hamburg's art scene—including Anna Oppermann and Herbert Hossmann—to develop an exhibition project titled *Eremit? Forscher? Sozialarbeiter? Das veränderte Selbstverständnis von Künstlern* (Hermit? Researcher? Social Worker? Artists' Changed Understanding of Themselves). In the summer of 1979, this group show examined the elementary conditions needed for producing art and questioned the social relevance of art.[13] Preceding the concept is a question about the way artists understand themselves: "Are artists today hermits? Researchers? Social workers?" In the catalogue accompanying the show, Oppermann leaves open the space provided for a photograph of the artist in her studio, stating, "Photo missing, since there is no studio."[14]

Oppermann was not able to separate her work and living space, and so her ensembles sprawled out into the rooms of the apartment in Rutschbahn that she had been sharing with her partner Herbert Hossmann since 1977. Hossmann, a publisher of art books who had close friendships with many artists, helped Dieter Roth with one of his pieces. Every day for a year, Roth sent Hossmann the flattened rubbish he gathered. Hossmann organized and archived them

12 The German term *Spurensicherung* can be translated as "to secure traces" and was made up in 1974 by the art historian Günter Metken. Metken emphasizes the fascination of certain artists for historical traces. Their art was on one hand inspired by methods of archaeologists and forensic researchers and on the other hand imbedded a critique on scientific inquiry.

13 See Elke Bippus, "Forschen in der Kunst. Anna Oppermann's Modell der Welterschließung," in Vorkoeper 2007, p. 55.

14 Quoted in Uwe M. Schneede, ed, *Eremit? Forscher? Sozialarbeiter? Das veränderte Selbstverständnis von Künstlern*, exh. cat., Kunstverein und Kunsthaus Hamburg (Hamburg, 1979), p. 64.

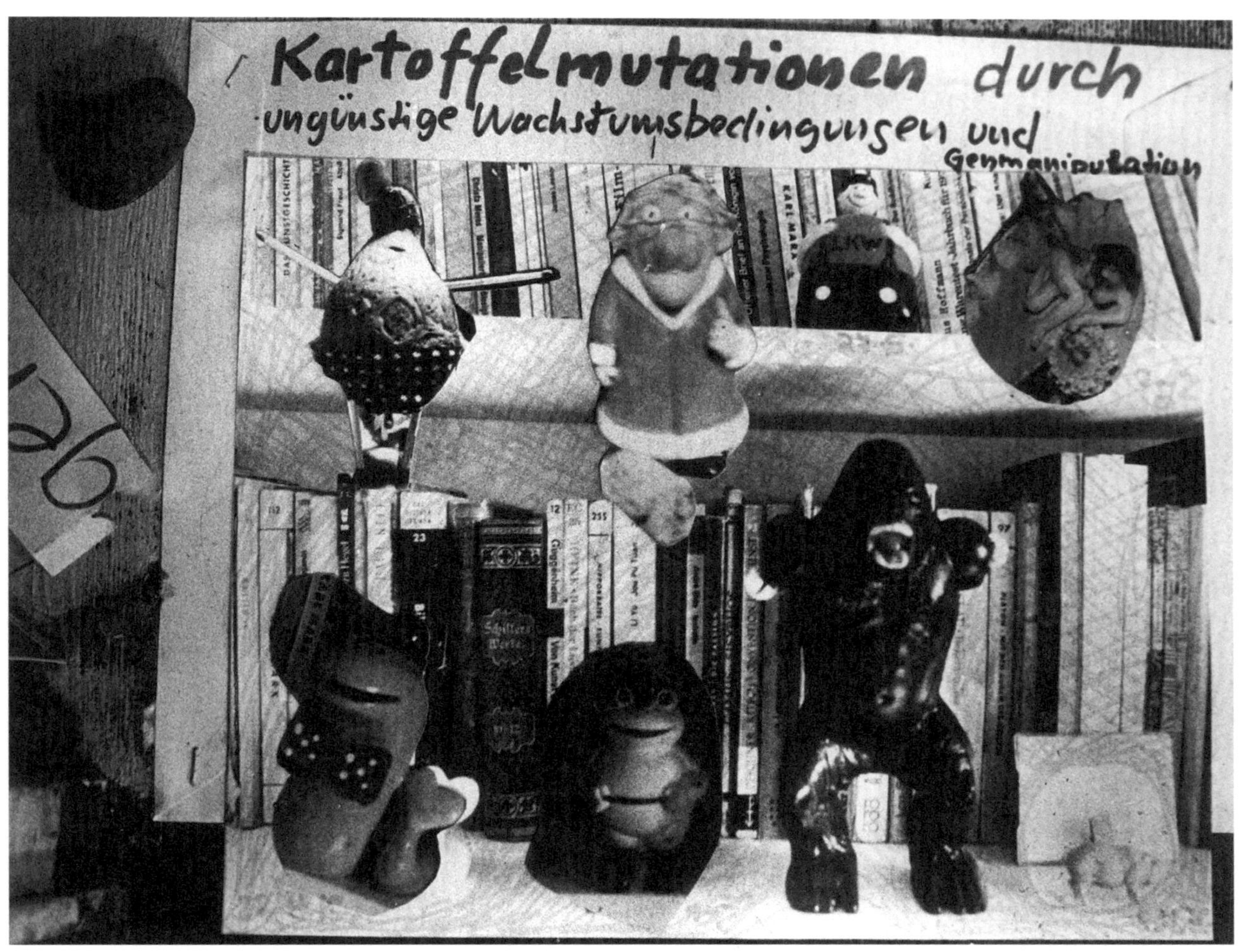

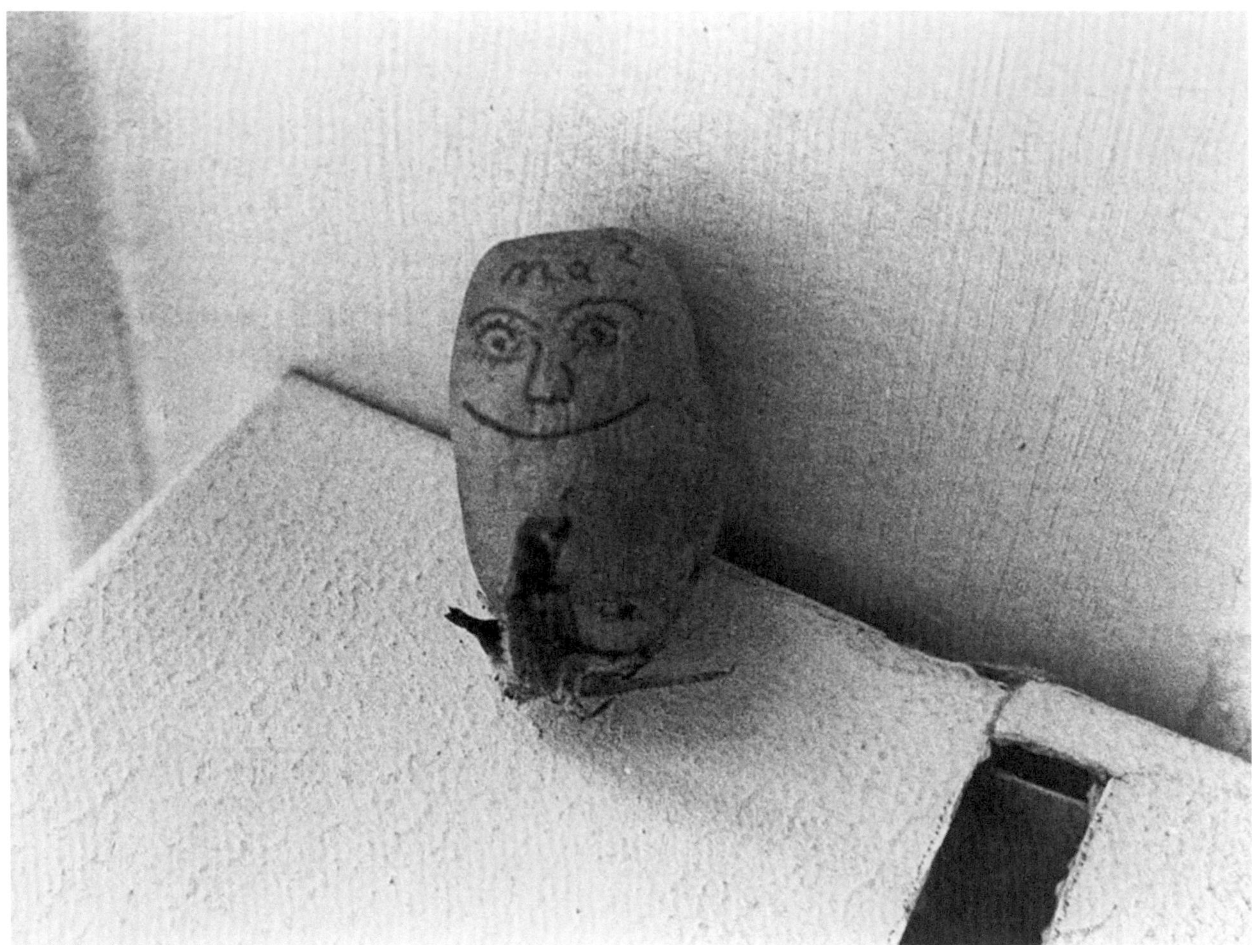

FIGS. 16, 17 Photographs by Anna Oppermann.

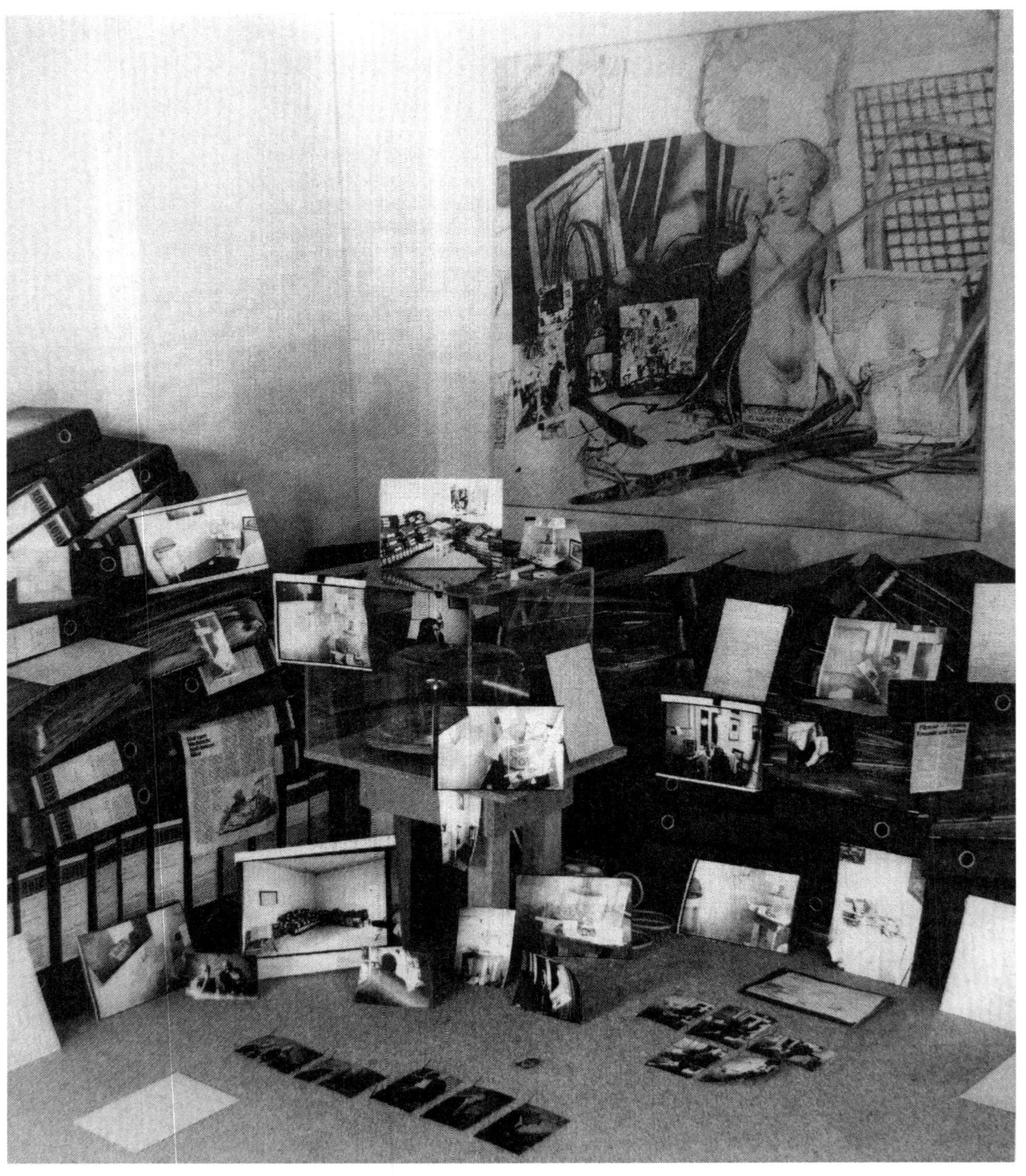

FIG. 18 Anna Oppermann, *Käse und Mäuse* (Cheese and Mouse), 1978, amid Dieter Roth's *Flacher Abfall* (Flat Rubbish), 1975–76. Filing cabinet with rubbish inside plastic files.

in transparent plastic and then assembled them in binders. Soon Roth's materials were piled up in a corner of the flat, which irritated Oppermann, who needed the space for her own work. She worked through her anger in the ensemble *Käse und Mäuse* (Cheese and Mouse, 1978). She was firmly convinced that storing Roth's work attracted vermin, which in turn endangered her ensemble pieces.[15] After the project *Flacher Abfall* (Flat Rubbish, 1975–76) was completed, the archive contained 800 file folders full of Roth's trash.[16]

Various exhibitions of the era explored the changing self-image of the artist, which was different from that of modern artists, since the artist no longer appeared in the social network as a utopian, an innovator, or a seismograph. In an attempt to shape a new concept of public life that would also count the previously disregarded tasks automatically relegated to women, such as housework, reproduction, and childcare, as a visible service to society, women artists and theorists advocated for upgrading the work of family reproduction as salaried work, which should be met with the appropriate financial and social remuneration.

The extremely critical, even distrustful, questioning of existing circumstances, of their own lives, and of being complicit, led to a deconstruction of the subject and a general insecurity around being able to formulate statements about "reality." The artist-subject's identity crisis and the discourse concerning the death of the author took place during the birth and early years of second wave feminism and the strengthening of feminist criticism, and the new reality of life for women took up the rallying cry: "The personal is political."

—Translated by Allison Moseley

15 See Vorkoeper 2007, p. 233.

16 See Dietmar Rübel, "Abfall – Materialien einer Archäologie des Konsums oder: Kunst vom Rest der Welt," in Monika Wagner, ed., *Material in Kunst und Alltag*, (Berlin: De Gruyter, 2002), p. 136, footnote 23.

Checklist

Unless otherwise noted all works courtesy Anna Oppermann Estate, Galerie Barbara Thumm, Berlin.

Works not in the exhibition are marked with a †.

p. 27 *Beans*, 1968
Mixed media on Masonite
43 ¼ × 43 ¼ inches
(110 × 110 cm)

p. 29 *Chives*, 1968
Mixed media on Masonite
43 ¾ × 44 inches
(111 × 112 cm)

p. 31 *Untitled*, 1969
Mixed media on Masonite
51 × 47 ¼ inches
(130 × 120)

p. 33 *Red figure with curtain*, 1968
Mixed media on Masonite
59 × 48 inches
(150 × 122 cm)

p. 35 *Mirror corner*, 1968/1970
Mixed media on Masonite
51 ⅛ × 54 ¼ inches
(130 × 138 cm)

p. 37 *With ashtray*, 1968/1970
Part of the ensemble "Antidesign"
Mixed media on Masonite
59 × 48 inches (150 × 122 cm)

p. 39 *Untitled*, 1970
Mixed media on cardboard
32 ½ × 23 ¼ inches
(83 × 59 cm)

p. 41 *Untitled*, 1970
Mixed media on cardboard
33 × 23 ¼ inches
(84 × 59 cm)

p. 43 *Untitled*, 1970
Mixed media on cardboard
33 × 23 ¼ inches
(84 × 59 cm)

p. 45 *Untitled*, ca. 1968
Mixed media on cardboard
19 ¾ × 33 inches (50 × 84 cm)

p. 47 *Untitled*, ca. 1968/1970
Mixed media on cardboard
33 × 23 ¼ inches
(84 × 59 cm)

p. 49 *Untitled*, 1970
Mixed media on cardboard
33 × 23 ½ inches
(84 × 60 cm)
Courtesy Tim Phillips, Boston, MA.

p. 51 *Untitled*, ca. 1968
Mixed media on cardboard
32 ¾ × 23 ¼ inches
(83.5 × 59 cm)

p. 53 *Untitled*, ca. 1968
Mixed media on cardboard
31 × 23 ¾ inchess
(78.5 × 60 cm)

p. 55 *Untitled*, before 1968
Mixed media on cardboard
22 × 20 inches (56 × 52 cm)

p. 57 *Table with round views*, 1968
Mixed media on cardboard
78 ¾ × 39 ¼ inches
(200 × 100 cm)

p. 59 *Being a Housewife*, 1968/1973
Mixed media
Dimensions variable

p. 61 † *Untitled*, 1969/1970
Mixed technique on Masonite
59 × 48 inches (150 × 122 cm)

p. 63 † *Untitled*, ca. 1968
Mixed media on cardboard
33 × 19 ¾ inches (84 × 50 cm)

p. 65 † *Indian girl*, 1971
Colored pencil on Masonite
59 × 48 inches (150 × 122 cm)
Signed and dated "A.O. 1971"

p. 67 † *Untitled*, ca. 1965/1968
Mixed media on Masonite
39 ¾ × 39 ¼ inches
(101.3 × 100 cm)

p. 69 † *Untitled*, ca. 1965/1968
Mixed media on Masonite
39 ½ × 39 ¼ inches
(100.2 × 99.7 cm)

p. 71 † *Untitled*, ca. 1965/1968
Mixed media on Masonite
39 ¼ × 39 ¾ inches
(100 × 101 cm)

p. 73 † *Untitled*, ca. 1965/1968
Mixed media on Masonite
39 ¼ × 39 ¼ inches
(100 × 100 cm)

p. 75 † *Untitled*, ca. 1965/1968
Mixed media on Masonite
39 ¼ × 39 ¼ inches
(100 × 100 cm)

p. 77 † *Untitled (Picture!)*, 1970
Lithograph
32 ¾ × 23 ¼ inches
(83 × 59 cm)
Edition 100 + 1 E.A.

p. 79 † *Untitled*, 1973
Lithograph
24 ¾ × 31 ½ inches framed
(63.2 × 80.2 cm)

p. 81 † *Lithography (Beans)*, 1974
Lithograph
22 × 30 inches
(56.2 × 76.2 cm)

p. 83 † *The closest thing*, 1974
Lithograph
29 ¾ × 22 ¼ inches framed
(75.6 × 56.6 cm)

Acknowledgments

For a relatively small exhibition, this project has been in the works for quite some time. Since encountering Anna Oppermann's drawings nearly a decade ago, I've wanted to organize an exhibition of her work. Galerie Barbara Thumm represents the Anna Oppermann Estate, and Barbara Thumm has been a fellow traveler, cheerleader, fixer, interlocutor, and a champion of finding a wider audience for Oppermann's work. I could not have organized this exhibition without her generous assistance. Alex Oppermann, Anna Oppermann's son, trusted me with his mother's work and provided valuable insight into her practice. I'm grateful for his support and his participation in the organization of the exhibition. Catalog contributor Ute Vorkoeper, who wrote her dissertation on Oppermann's work and assisted the artist toward the end of her life, shared her deep knowledge of Oppermann's art as well as her analysis and interpretation. I am thankful for her scholarship and previous exhibitions on which ours builds, and for the care she took installing *Being a Housewife* at the Carpenter Center. Meta Marina Beeck, assistant curator at Kunsthalle Bielefeld, who spent many hours in the artist's archives, generously allowed a version of her essay, originally written for the recent Bielefeld Oppermann exhibition, to be translated for our catalogue. Chief Curator at the Hammer Museum at UCLA, Connie Butler (who I found out early in my research process was already an Oppermann fan) made time in a very busy schedule to write a beautiful new text. I'm grateful. Thanks also go to Friedrich Meschede, director of the Kunsthalle Bielefeld, who was a one-time collaborator on this project, and who organized an important show of Oppermann's work around the same time as the Carpenter Center's.

Editor Eugenia Bell helped shape the texts and brought an elegant, precise coherence to all the book's contents. This is the fifth book I've made with the excellent designer Chad Kloepfer, and his first for the Carpenter Center. It may be my favorite yet. Julia Featheringill and Stewart Clements produced pitch-perfect installation photography. We thank Allison Moseley for her translation of Meta Marina Beeck's text.

The Carpenter Center for the Visual Arts has a small staff for the ambition of its projects. Our exhibitions are expertly organized by Exhibitions Manager/Registrar Anna Kovacs (who can tame even the most complex project). Anna is aided by our highly capable Exhibitions

Production Assistant Katie Soule. Former Assistant Director Daisy Nam contributed to the organization of this exhibition, and indeed contributed in countless essential ways to most functions of the Carpenter Center. Curatorial Fellow and Art, Film, and Visual Studies PhD student Carolyn Bailey provided insight and excellent coordination for this publication. Essential support was also provided by colleagues in the department of Art, Film, and Visual Studies, including Department Chair and Professor Robb Moss, Finance Manager Mary Park, Staff Assistant Laura Sargent, and, the endlessly supportive Denise Oberdan, Director of Administration.

This book marks the first in a series of collaborations between the Carpenter Center and publisher Inventory Press: ideal partners who ensured that the book reflects their considerable expertise and smarts. Thanks to Shannon Harvey, Adam Michaels, and Matteo Cossu.

I'm grateful to the Anna Oppermann Estate and Boston collector Tim Phillips for lending their works to the exhibition. Finally, a thank you to Anna Oppermann, an artist I sadly never met, but whose work has inspired me for nearly a decade, and will continue to encourage me—and those who see it—to radically reimagine the relationships between one's inner life and objects, spaces, and language that structure everything around us.

—*Dan Byers*
John R. and Barbara Robinson Family Director

Contributors

META MARINA BEECK is an art historian and curator. She studied art history and German literature at Humboldt University in Berlin, and Chinese language at Peking University, in Beijing. Since 2015, Beeck has held the position of assistant curator at Kunsthalle Bielefeld, in Bielefeld, Germany.

CONNIE BUTLER is chief curator at the Hammer Museum in Los Angeles. Previously she served as the Robert Lehman Foundation Chief Curator of Drawings at the Museum of Modern Art, New York, and as curator at the Museum of Contemporary Art, Los Angeles.

DAN BYERS is John R. and Barbara Robinson Family Director of the Carpenter Center for the Visual Arts and Lecturer in the Department of Art, Film, and Visual Studies at Harvard University. Previously he was Mannion Family Senior Curator at the ICA/Boston, and Co-Curator of the 2013 Carnegie International.

UTE VORKOEPER is an artist, art historian, and the curator for the Anna Oppermann Estate. She was the curator of the first posthumous retrospectives of Oppermann's ensemble works.

Reproduction Credits

With the exception of the following, all images are courtesy Anna Oppermann Estate and Galerie Barbara Thumm, Berlin, Germany

p. 18 © Chantal Akerman Foundation; courtesy Collection Cinematek.

p. 21 © 2019 Artists Rights Society (ARS), New York / VG Bild-Kunst, Bonn / documenta archive; photo: Dieter Schwerdtle

p. 92 Courtesy Tim Phillips, Boston, MA

p. 104 (top) Courtesy Alexander Oppermann

p. 106 © 2019 Artists Rights Society (ARS), New York / Bildrecht, Vienna; courtesy Berlinische Galerie

pp. 115 © 2019 documenta archive; photo: Hans-Kurt Boehlke

p. 118 © 2019 Artbrokerdesign; photo: Joop Schot

p. 119 © 2019 Maria Lassnig Foundation / Artists Rights Society (ARS), New York / VG Bild-Kunst, Bonn / The Albertina Museum, Vienna